Revisioning War Trauma in Cinema

Psychoanalytic Studies: Clinical, Social, and Cultural Contexts

Series Editor

Michael O'Loughlin, Adelphi University

Mission Statement

Psychoanalytic Studies seeks psychoanalytically informed works addressing the implications of the location of the individual in clinical, social, cultural, historical, and ideological contexts. Innovative theoretical and clinical works within psychoanalytic theory and in fields such as anthropology, education, and history are welcome. Projects addressing conflict, migrations, difference, ideology, subjectivity, memory, psychiatric suffering, physical and symbolic violence, power, and the future of psychoanalysis itself are welcome, as are works illustrating critical and activist applications of clinical work.

See https://rowman.com/Action/SERIES/LEX/LEXPS for a list of advisory board members.

Titles in the Series

Revisioning War Trauma in Cinema: Uncoming Communities, by Jessica Datema and Manya Steinkoler

Women & Psychosis: Multidisciplinary Perspectives, edited by Marie Brown and Marilyn Charles

Psychoanalysis from the Indian Terroir: Emerging Themes in Culture, Family, and Childhood in India, edited by Manasi Kumar, Anup Dhar, and Anurag Mishra

A Three-Factor Model of Couples Psychotherapy: Projective Identification, Level of Couple Object Relations, and Omnipotent Control, by Robert Mendelsohn

Revisioning War Trauma in Cinema

Uncoming Communities

Jessica Datema and Manya Steinkoler

LEXINGTON BOOKS
Lanham • Boulder • New York • London

Published by Lexington Books
An imprint of The Rowman & Littlefield Publishing Group, Inc.
4501 Forbes Boulevard, Suite 200, Lanham, Maryland 20706
www.rowman.com

6 Tinworth Street, London SE11 5AL

British Library Cataloguing in Publication Information Available

Library of Congress Cataloging-in-Publication Data

Names: Datema, Jessica, author. | Steinkoler, Manya.
Title: Revisioning war trauma in cinema : uncoming communities / Jessica Datema and Manya Steinkoler.
Description: Lanham : Lexington Books, 2019. | Includes bibliographical references and index.
Identifiers: : LCCN 2019001746 (print) | LCCN 2019009241 (ebook) | ISBN 9781498592987 (Electronic) | ISBN 9781498592970 (hbk.)
Subjects: LCSH: War films--History and criticism. | Psychic trauma in motion pictures. | Suffering in motion pictures.
Classification: LCC PN1995.9.W3 (ebook) | LCC PN1995.9.W3 D34 2019 (print) | DDC 791.43/6581--dc23
LC record available at https://lccn.loc.gov/2019001746

Contents

Acknowledgments

This book began as articles on films. Some chapters were previously published or presented at psychoanalytic conferences, including *Das Unbehagen* in New York City and *Le regard qui bat* in Paris. We are deeply grateful and indebted to the many colleagues and intellectual companions that have helped shape the spirit and insights of this project, including David Lichtenstein, Todd McGowan, and J. J. Moskovitz. Also, we are grateful to Jay Datema for his incalculable editorial prowess. To quote James Joyce, without all this help there would be "no pen, no ink, no table, no room, no time, no quiet, no inclination," and simply no book. Thank you to Max Richter for providing sonic inspiration. Finally, we dedicate this book to "the unknown, or initiates that Georges Bataille (at least once) will call 'the negative community,' [to] the community of those who have no community."[1] All articles were co-written except chapters 5 and 6, which were solely written by Dr. Datema, and chapter 7, which was written by Dr. Steinkoler.

NOTE

1. Maurice Blanchot, *The Unavowable Community* (Barrytown, NY: Station Hill, 1988).

Introduction

Cinema of the Uncoming

Jean-Luc Godard famously claimed that "cinema had failed to show the Holocaust" and saw this as a moral failure.[1] *Revisioning War Trauma in Cinema: Uncoming Communities* responds to this claim and alerts us to the ways cinema can, to quote Samuel Beckett, fail better. The book examines films that concern war trauma and its aftermath to show how *trauma*, from the Greek word "to make a hole," is a potential site of invention. This traumatic notion of a hole concerns the invention of subjectivity; all subsequent traumas harken to the trauma of being in language—that is, they invoke the creation of this initial, archaic hole. The films we treat show how the tear in the fabric of reality that emerges through trauma can serve as an opportunity for creation. Perhaps cinema still "fails to show the Holocaust," but that does not mean that it cannot reveal something of the mystery of showing itself, making art convey a glimpse of the void at its source.

Revisioning War Trauma in Cinema reflects on films that invent rather than represent at the very instance history breaks down. We make use of psychoanalytic theory since it provides a framework and a robust language that allows us to speak about what evades sense, as well as to foreground an aesthetics and politics of difference. Our book mobilizes philosophical as well as psychoanalytic theories of trauma and community that are not based on consensus or excess[2] but on construction and invention. Psychoanalytic theory allows us to realize that art may be a way of ciphering the real in the same way that the unconscious does; it makes something where there was nothing. This approach follows what Mari Ruti claims is the task of theory, namely "to reveal previously unrecognized possibilities (for life, desire, action, thought, the imagination, and so on)—possibilities that are not always realizable in the 'real' world but that cause us to see differently."[3] The book uses theory to critically examine films that take up this project of "seeing differently." These films show how art, in particular cinema, is one way to bear the unbearable, or what Lacan calls the real that resists representation.

Close readings of these films show how cinema, as an art form, can have an intimate and particular relation to trauma since the screen accommodates the emergence of what history fails to transmit. As Cathy Caruth contends, "For history to be a history of trauma means that it is referential precisely to the extent that it is not fully perceived as it occurs, or to put it somewhat differently, that a history can be grasped only in the very inaccessibility of its occurrence."[4] *Revisioning War Trauma* takes up the impossible task of *re-visioning* at the point where representation breaks down, screening an impossible memory where a historic void threatens to destroy both ego and subject, character and culture. The screen allows for a testimonial of "scribblings," or what Maurice Blanchot calls "literature, [which] by its very activity, denies the substance of what it represents."[5] Reflecting this language at the border of meaning, *Revisioning War Trauma* examines films that visualize the non-representational placelessness of trauma.

This book explores films that show the fallout of history and the failure of the social order as a consequence of the imaginary injunctions of the nation-state or the demands for group cohesion and identity. As with psychoanalytic trauma theory, beginning with Freud, Blanchot's ideas of community and art are founded on poetic invention out of disaster, paradox, and impossibility. The subtitle, *Uncoming Communities*, concerns Maurice Blanchot's idea of a community of uncommon Others or exiles, war-torn figures who can never be returned to culture as they knew it; they can never go home and remain in a state of perpetual non-arrival. Their kinship is not based on interpretive rituals *in common*—practices that would buttress Kant's Enlightenment notion of *sensus communis* that grounds universalist aesthetics. Rather, *Uncoming Communities* denotes an uncommon linkage of figures surviving war trauma and disaster, figures who find an uncanny kinship based on their exile and pariahdom.

"Uncoming communities" in films that revision war trauma are founded on a confrontation with death and the hole that trauma exposes. "Coming" is a cultural injunction, a demand to become. By "coming" we mean obeying the super-egoic demand to enjoy as well as indulging in narcissistic cultural ideals that messianically promise a fullness of being always in the future. We build the subtitle from the word "uncoming" as a resistance to *jouissance*, and as a limit to the cultural demands for "coming."[6] The uncoming also refers to the traumatic departure of figures in our films from their homes and their symbolic places; they are always in the process of departing, embodying the hemorrhaging of any imaginary consistency that belonging compels.

This Blanchotian being, this exile, the founding figure of uncoming communities, emerges out of historic trauma as an exceptional force opposing cultural belonging, development, imaginary group identity, and ideology. The protagonists in the films set themselves apart from demands like "Be all you can be" or "Keep it coming," resisting the cultural super-egoic excess of demand. Linked by the breakdown of community, the figures in these films cannot go home and their dreams are no longer possible. Unlike the Hollywood promise of happy ending in *Field of Dreams*, where "if you build it, they will come," in the scorched landscape of postwar cinema, no one is left to come, and every edifice—even the very possibility of address, of calling the Other to come—has been destroyed. Uncoming implies that there is never arrival or closure after war trauma, only departure.

The "un" in "uncoming" literally refers to the creation of a separation and refusal to engage the excess of enjoyment. Figures in these films inaugurate uncoming communities that withstand traumatic excess by founding unfamiliar threads of income, welcome, and outcome: for example, Saul's attempt at construction of a funeral in *Son of Saul* to welcome the next generation; or Hannah Arendt's welcoming of American students and controversial friendship with Mary McCarthy as a German exile; or the Argentinian hotel in *The German Doctor* where Enzo and his family set up business and eventually demand that Mengele leave; or the killing of the unwanted guest in *The Beguiled*—all exemplify different forms of income, welcome, and outcome toward the refugee and stranger.

Revisioning War Trauma is not based on unanimity but is stumbled upon through cinematic inventions and interventions: letters, scribblings, and graphic songs, like what Blanchot calls "a writing of the disaster."[7] As a departure from consensus-society and as withdrawal from ideology, the films in this collection do not try to "make sense" of trauma. Instead, uncoming communities are bound by "community, in its very failure [which] is linked to a certain kind of writing, a writing that has nothing else to search for than the last words."[8] This type of community that is founded upon failure is inaugurated by figures who search for the "last words." This is seen, for example, in Christian Petzold's *Phoenix*, when the Berlin nightclub star Nelly, like the mythic phoenix, returns to the city having survived the concentration camp, singing Kurt Weill's "Speak Low" to the very people who sent her there. The myriad meanings that "speaking low" conveys—as under the radar, not registered, not direct, from beneath—serve as the last word that makes the film the phoenix it is named. Nelly's singing is the graphic scribbling or intervention that allows her to rise from the ashes.

The films we consider are a testament to the human capacity to survive catastrophe, not by representation or interpretation, but via construction.[9] We learn from trauma studies that trauma can never be directly remembered and requires indirect modes of healing. In a 1938 essay titled "Constructions in

Analysis," Freud defines construction as distinct from interpretation. He explains "construction" as a modality of psychoanalytic intervention that differs from interpretation: "Interpretation applies to something that one does to some single element of the material, such as an association or a parapraxis. But it is a 'construction' when one lays before the subject of the analysis a piece of his early history that he has forgotten."[10] Construction is a way of not only figuring a forgotten history, but of preserving what was lost or what could never be remembered. The films we discuss use construction as a method of inventive revisioning that involves "re-membering," which means allowing truth to be made rather than interpreted. In this manner, the films follow Freud in allowing a constructed truth regarding trauma to emerge affectively and even unintentionally.

As artworks, these films make use of Freud's clinical advancement. Freud remarked of constructions in analysis: "so little is said about 'constructions,' . . . because 'interpretations' and their effects are spoken of instead. But I think that 'construction' is by far the more appropriate description."[11] Freud is describing something of the way the analyst contributes to the invention of the past. These remarks at the end of his career concern the analyst's act, a term Lacan used to explain "the setting into act of the subject" and "the setting into act of the unconscious."[12] For Freud, the construction was an act of the analyst arising by way of the analytic work as an invention, not an interpretation. As construction, these films offer a supplement to meaning where previously there had been only a void, or layers of worn out interpretations.

Importantly, Freud comes to this understanding at the end of his life after years of clinical work that used interpretation as a primary method. By way of construction, the trauma, the forgotten, and the real are ushered to the fore. Said differently, a construction surfaces "the search for the last word" of trauma to come to terms with the interminable, allowing something unexpected to take form, to come to life. Like late Freudian analytic work with construction, art invents by way of the real and the unconscious rather than via interpretation. In the films we discuss, as with construction, the direction is less toward interpretive knowing than it is a means of bringing to the screen what was lost to memory. Rather than neurotically trying to make repression "work" in the name of an ideal, the films use the forgetting inherent to mental life, and in particular to trauma, to show what has occurred and has left traces but could not be recorded. A failure of memory then becomes re-membered or re-visioned as an artistic or analytic possibility.

The films foreground the failed repression as resulting from a history fragmented by trauma. Cinematic art here becomes a kind of testimony that includes and makes use of the very mechanisms that history as narrative cannot bear and to which it has no access. It testifies to a traumatic history, which resists knowing, memory, and interpretation. These films show that the Holocaust is what cannot be shown, but the Holocaust is what perpetually gives rise to showing: the real of trauma is the very source of art as construction.

In addition to being representative of the Freudian notions of construction, these films could be described as "Sinthomatic" in Lacanian terms. Lacan's Sinthome theorized in *Seminar XXIII* (1975–1976) concerns a savoir faire with the void as a way of inventing, negotiating, and commemorating.[13] This is a savoir faire that allows the refugee or exile to create in the aftermath of war, where history and often place is catastrophically erased. The filmic screen functions as an artistic supplement, something like Lacan's fourth ring that helps tie reality back together, albeit differently. The screen does not just record, but welcomes the unexpected, allowing new narratives to emerge that revision the very wounds that make art necessary in the first place. With one exception that we highlight, the films we analyze function as Sinthomatic constructions of (subjective) history in the breakdown of the social and historic orders that allow the world to consist once again. This invention, coming in the place of symbolic failure, allows subjectivity to sustain itself in front of the real that continually threatens to destroy it.

Lacan's *Seminar XXIII* invents the "Sinthome" to indicate the knots of subjectivity, which bind even without what Lacan calls the Name-of-the-Father. This is made possible via an artistic creation or construction that signifies the real by ciphering *jouissance*. The Name-of-the-Father was one way Lacan understood the metaphorization of the desire of the mother by language, a way that in neurosis allows meaning to become grounded in an originary loss and reality structured in and by language. It is a function lacking in psychosis and often in perversion, and unraveled in traumatic experience that collapses history. The Sinthome is the way these films rename history as traumatic construction. Thus, the films are "another way to name it [history], and that's why today I'm covering what there is of the Name-of-the-Father at the level at which Joyce testifies to it—which deserves to be called the Sinthome."[14] The films do not draw back from exposing the moment when traditional rituals, which bind the social order, fail and make use of the screen as a weft for traumatic *jouissance*. In this sense, we could say the films themselves are Blanchotian artistic constructions born from a savoir faire with *jouissance*, and an invention out of disaster.[15]

Like Freud's founding of the notion of construction later in his work, Lacan's formulation of the Sinthome, while a new moment in his theory, was the culmination of his psychoanalyzing *against* interpretation. Lacan's resistance to interpretation is well known, as is his invention of the analytic act aimed at the patient's *jouissance*, a technique for dealing with stasis in the treatment. By way of the Sinthome, rather than interpreting, the subject identifies with the Sinthome; the subject enjoys his unconscious. Here there is a kind of separation at work where the subject is no longer plagued by the drive or by cultural demands. Some of these ideas about a how-to-do with *jouissance* that are presented in Lacan's later seminars appeared in an earlier form in *Seminar XI* where "*se parer*"—to give birth to oneself—is considered what would take place "after" the symptom.[16] For after the meaning of the symptom is emptied out, the Sinthome holds the *jouissance* that had once been bound to meaning or to meaning's future.

The Sinthome is a transformation of some of the desire that plagued the subject in the symptom, but one in which the subject is not duped since he created it himself, and not one wherein he is bothered, since the excess is the source of his creation. The Sinthome invents a new signifier imbued with *jouissance*, *ex nihilo*, out of nothing. By *ex nihilo* we mean both the literal "out of nothing," but also the Sinthomatic sense of creating from a "hole," that is the real of trauma. As such, the Sinthome supposes a *savoir faire* with *jouissance* and handling of the *ex nihilo* where the real of trauma becomes the very void that is the motor of creation. Instead of interpreting war trauma as a symptom, the films in this book construct via Sinthome as a cure, not to represent what happened, but to construct uncoming communities.

The Lacanian Sinthome, like Freudian construction, permits a supplemental history to arise where an understood or accepted history has been rendered null and void by catastrophe. Sinthomatic constructions are like what Blanchot calls the "search for the last word" and a means of cinematic revisioning as screening the *hole* of trauma. They cull the void for treasure, for the emergence of an unforeseen. Such cinematic constructions not only concern an unremembered past, but partake of, and work on, the impasses and tensions of our own historic moment. They alert us to the fact that histories are always ideological and dependent on a field of vision. *Revisioning War Trauma in Cinema* challenges us to "see differently" by revisioning or seizing hold of testimonies that articulate a reality outside conventional, canonical narratives.

While critical theory helps us look at films nowadays furnishing us with a new critical vocabulary, historically myth handled the real bringing the real to culture prior to the written word. In this sense, myth like Blanchot's "last word" is always already a "first word." Rather than representing historical facts, the films' language constructs mythically in a more direct engagement. Myth functions where interpretation cannot, since like construction, it is a way to symbolize what resists symbolization since myth is the way storytelling can bear infinity. It involves a savoir-faire with the hole. This sort of artistic construction is located at the border between the oral and the written, the void and the word, at the juncture of representation and the *ex-nihilo*, absence and presence. All of the films use myth since myth is a way of working with non-representation. In *Phoenix* Nelly rises out of the concentration camp ashes; in *The German Doctor* Lilith and her mother make a monstrous creation scene; in *The Beguiled*, the Demeter Persephone myth is reenacted by the characters. It is not simply that the films use myth, but they reconstruct and reenact the myths they use.

Instead of recognition or identification, war wounds and scars suture the figures in the films who bear markings beyond recognition that are the beginning of invention. The figures are made distinct by their scars and war wounds, which expose at once their fragility and possibility. We see this with the twins in *The German Doctor*, the raped body of Anonyma in *Woman in Berlin*, Nelly's camp number in *Phoenix*, or Saul's in *Son of Saul*. Their scars bind the traumatic excess to avoid both the narcissistic pitfalls of melancholia as well as the satisfactions of the death drive. Changed on the level of the body by their scars, uncoming characters' wounds keep them from being reduced to any particular cultural or universalizing imaginary. Like myth, scars provide a form of extra-symbolic "wreck-cognition."

Figures in the films have been citizens of authoritarian societies, which, like the ancient myths, still reflect and engage issues facing us today. Simultaneously challenging historical ideology, as well as contemporary neoliberal discourse, figures in the films survive war trauma and stand in opposition to political excess. They show how the breakdown of citizenship that occurs after being subject to an authoritarian common cause or a perverse ideal of the common can simultaneously serve as the beginning of a construction. They struggle to remain human despite severe alienation under embattled circumstances that threaten their social ties and often their lives.

Their alienation, when subjected to an ideal, may persist all the way to a confrontation with death. This persistence may inaugurate a negative, unavowable community not based on common ideals or consensus but upon "the death of those one calls, maybe mistakenly, its members."[17] Blanchot's work provides powerful thought on the intimate relation of community to art, death, exile, and the Other. Community is not only the sharing of speech, but a relation to the traumatic unsaid—that is, an unavowable, mythic potential that comes through the "absence of community."[18] For Blanchot, the community is founded upon a negation integral to it, namely the absent Other, or those not represented.

This absent Other exists as exempt from the very imaginary certitude that is erroneously thought to found community. Maurice Blanchot himself lived through the rise of fascism and witnessed the problematization of shared fantasy as contributing. Figures in the films face war and death to forge a different type of bond and construct "a community [that] is the presentation to its members of their mortal truth. It is the presentation of finitude and of excess without possibility of return that founds the finite-being."[19] Their kinship is an exposure to death, which functions as a yoking foundational exposure. A traumatic hole becomes the foundation, the inauguration, the very opening of community. All the protagonists in the films, including Nelly, Saul, Maria Altmann, and Anonyma, confront a mortal truth that is the opposite of imaginary certitude. Uncoming communities, like Blanchot's *Unavowable Community*, engage an existential mortal truth not to be repudiated but engaged.

Instead of dreaming, uncoming figures engage in the Heideggerian act of building, dwelling, and thinking in the diaspora, living without assurance in the fallout of catastrophe. This is the creative work of construction that pertains to bare existence. The filmic figures work on an existential level to continue being by "not being there" after having been erased. This work involves a subjective construction that is often mythopoetic. It is an invention through the dialectic of presence and absence that regards being. This dialectic is illustrated in what Gertrude Stein wrote about in *Everybody's Autobiography* regarding Oakland, that "there is no there there."[20] Having survived and written in the aftermath of both world wars, Stein's simultaneous anonymity and universality is part of her mythopoetic invention *ex nihilo*. Like figures in the films, Stein uses anonymity and an autobiographical pseudonym to think, dwell, and create in a state of "not being there." Moreover, after fleeing Paris during World War II, Gertrude Stein and Alice B. Toklas continued their artistic lives, surviving precisely by exiling themselves, a historical fact often ignored by critics.

Like the Lost Generation, *Revisioning War Trauma in Cinema: Uncoming Communities* features figures who survive, paradoxically, by inventing while "not being there." They participate in a logic of dis-appearance that goes against cultural attempts to monitor human "thereness." Today, imaginary mandates to police cultural "thereness" persist, as for example, in paranoiac responses to refugees from over "there" coming here, or in the continuous use of technology that is always "there" to "protect." The policing of immigrants and the acceleration of invasive societal technology, which is alive and well today, has not prevented more terrorist attacks or hacking. Rather, in America's late capital culture of bio-power and excess, consumption drives *jouissance*, demanding lack be filled by any "there." Contrarily, figures in these films resist covering over their lack and suffer confrontation with the real. They epitomize the individual emerging from imaginary bonds in common, into uncoming communities of abject invention.

In his "Theses on the Philosophy of History," Walter Benjamin claims that traditional historical narratives of progress cannot and have not presented the true disaster of history. For Benjamin, trauma can only be figured by nonrepresentational means—that is, in an artwork. In this sense, Benjamin's "Angelus Novus" illustrates the structure of the films as a whole, which show history not as a chain of events, but as "one single catastrophe which keeps piling wreckage upon wreckage and hurls it in front of his [the angel's] feet."[21] Klee's "Angelus Novus" is another way of thinking about how the war-traumatized figures in our book. As witnesses of "wreckage upon wreckage," these figures stand with one foot in death or their terrible past, and the other foot in life or a contingent future.

Much like Benjamin's use of Klee's painting to expose history as trauma, the films this book examines revision history like a phoenix rising from the ashes. Art makes use of myth to supplement the fact that "there is no document of civilization which is not at the same time a document of barbarism."[22] The films show a supplemental history through mythic and creative reinvention—that is, a creation that holds on to the real. Like Klee's "Angelus Novus," this book explores films that mark a phoenix rising and a departure from the cultural imaginary, which is often restrictive, demanding obedience.

Exposing mythic history, the protagonists in the films are transformed from citizen to scapegoat. Moreover, they remain the traumatic exception, or the perpetually cast out, much like what Giorgio Agamben calls "*Homo Sacer*."[23] This figure embodies the unassimilable as what remains in a state of perpetual exclusion from society, what Agamben calls "a legally unnamable and unclassifiable being."[24] It is by way of their sacred separation and non-sovereignty that the *Homo Sacer* figures in these films subsist. *Homo Sacer* refers not only to the narrative insofar as it concerns the exilic fate of the protagonists, but also to the level of the films themselves as art works.

Uncoming communities form around this scapegoat who is a reminder of what was forgotten on both a personal and political level. The mythic scapegoat reveals a tension that may have always existed but was repressed or bound before the trauma. This tension is between belonging as a citizen on the one hand and being subject to authoritarian control on the Other. It is sustained by the scapegoat as *Homo Sacer*—for example, what is separate, set apart, or what Agamben calls "bare life, abject in the double exclusion into which he [*Homo Sacer*] is taken, and [concerns] the violence to which he finds himself exposed."[25] Separated in this manner, figures in the films are not only cast out of society, but they are also subject to ongoing violence. Uncoming communities are composed of citizens whose bodies are reduced to bare life. Their identity is no longer a cultural given, nor is their future guaranteed by traditional notions of providence.

The films expose the prevalence of social antagonisms in the imaginary mandates of the state, including the struggles, pettiness, and hostility that accompany the nascent aggression in cultural demands for belonging. *Homo Sacer* exists at this "threshold of indeterminacy between democracy and absolutism.[26] This cast-out figure is emblematic of uncoming communities as freed from the escalating super-egoic demands of imaginary statehood. However, this is a vicious freedom that results in the condition of exile. *Homo Sacer* looms mythically as a banished figure of bare life in this juncture between democracy and absolutism. In the films, this figure becomes the stain of disaster and a constant force of testimony as exposure, whether recognized or not.

In our own moment, the *Homo Sacer* figure similarly exposes the breakdown of community that has been occluded by the regulatory functioning of norms. It makes an ethical presentation of history by exposing how bare "life—in its state of exception has now become the norm."[27] As such, like the war-torn figures, the films themselves impute the entire community. In addition to creating culpability as the stain that marks the social tie, characters in the films make use of this state of exception to survive as subjects. The films give human dignity to forms of subjective destitution through Sinthomatic construction.

Each chapter in *Revisioning* analyzes a film that shows the impossibility of community as formed by shared commonalities, but instead highlights the birth of subjectivity out of states of exception. As bodies reduced to bare existence, all the figures in the films engage a mortal truth as a result of being disinherited or exiled from their homeland. In Max Färberböck's *A Woman in Berlin* (2008), Anonyma is subject to the well-known but suppressed mass rape of German women by the Russians during the postwar occupation of Berlin. In Christian Petzold's *Phoenix*, Nelly returns from the camps with a reconstructed face only to find her disloyal husband and the surviving community a reminder of the mutual political and personal betrayal that led her to Auschwitz. In Lucia Puenzo's *The German Doctor* (2013), an Argentinian family unwittingly ends up being wounded by Josef Mengele after the women agree to "ameliorative" medical treatment that results in their bodily deformation. Maria Altmann is the exiled protagonist of Simon Curtis's *Woman in Gold* (2015) who petitions a legal claim to her family paintings hanging in the Belvedere museum after the Nazi annexation of Austria. In Margarethe von Trotta's *Hannah Arendt* (2012), the philosopher's own testimony regarding life as a Jewish refugee in America is juxtaposed with the trial of Adolf Eichmann. Florian Henckel von Donnersmarck's *The Lives of Others* (2006) shows the alienation of East German (GDR) citizenry through the Stasi officer Gerd Wiesler, who is more abject as a subject of ideology than the supposedly "officially" decadent playwright he observes. In László Nemes's *Son of Saul* (2015), Saul invents a son to bury and save a corpse from the crematoria since it is only by saving death that human dignity can be rescued from the flames. Finally, in Sofia Coppola's *The Beguiled*, Southern ladies, when confronted with the wounded Union soldier Corporal McBurney, castrate and kill him in an attempt to avoid confronting their own lack. We use this film as a counterexample to the other films, since here the community is "made" via regression as a resort to *jouissance* to prevent against lack and against the construction of a supplemental history.

Chapter one follows the wounded Anonyma, the incognito protagonist in *A Woman in Berlin* (2008) who decides, amidst the mass raping of German women, to seek protection from a Russian officer whom she elevates to a lover. In this way, she transforms victimhood into empowered choice. The film is an adaptation of the anonymous diary of the same woman, a German journalist, who provides firsthand testimony of the Russian invasion of Berlin. Like the diary upon which it is based, the film serves as a witness to her subjective reinvention out of catastrophe. Anonyma, an educated ex-journalist, writes about her own Nazi background prior to the Russian invasion, an irony that is reminiscent of the crimes of the German people. In the reduction to pure flesh and in her writing about it, Anonyma rejects recognition through naming. Despite the breakdown of her own national and social identity, as indicated by the fact that she remains anonymous, *A Woman in Berlin* relies on the dignity of storytelling to make narrative out of total lawlessness.

Chapter two analyzes Lucia Puenzo's *Wakolda*, or *The German Doctor* (2013), which is set in Argentina during the postwar period following the flight of Adolf Eichmann and Josef Mengele. We see the story through the eyes of a prepubescent girl whose family accidentally encounters Dr. Mengele, who is hiding under an assumed identity. The girl, as well as her pregnant mother, allows the mysterious doctor to experiment on them. These experiments promise their "rectification" from regular women into the German ideal. The guarantee of imaginary belonging is eventually exposed as bogus and dangerous when these women's bodies suffer the deleterious effects of Mengele's mad, monstrous "solution." While the women in the family initially succumb to the imaginary comforts of "belonging," Lilith ultimately ends up constructing her own story, which is the film itself. *The German Doctor* makes a creation myth by way of Lilith, named after the mythic woman who was cast out of paradise. Moreover, while mythic imagery constructs the film, it is also based on actual historical events. For example, the character Nora Eldoc, who was an Israeli spy and archivist, is based on an actual Holocaust survivor who, knowing the truth about Mengele, ended up dead. Nora intervenes to help Lilith separate from the doctor, as well as from her mother, and to construct the story itself. The film uses Lilith's account as a testimony of what was rubbed out of history concerning postwar Nazi activities in Argentina.

Chapter three analyzes Christian Petzold's film *Phoenix* (2015), which depicts a postwar birth out of the faceless ashes of death. The film invents life after death via art as an antidote to the famous Lanzmannian "sacred impossibility of representation."[28] Dramatically, this entails questioning and working through the temptations of perversion and nostalgia. The film narrates the intersection of a death camp survivor's unbearable history with postwar German survivor's guilt. The film's title, *Phoenix*, is a metaphor for both the film as artwork as well as for the haunting story of its protagonist. After her face is blown off in the camps, Nelly undergoes facial reconstructive surgery to return home to the husband who does not recognize her, and whom, she learns, had betrayed her to the Nazis. In returning from the camps, she literally rises from the ashes of her own faceless extermination. Her return to life, to Berlin, and to her husband is an unwelcome, unanticipated, uncanny interruption of postwar German assumptions. *Phoenix* shows a lone, courageous survivor of genocide, whose reappearance prefigures the alienated and disinherited refugees of our time; no one wants them to survive, to return, or to tell their stories. Their uncanny presence, like Nelly's, implicates us all.

Chapter four follows Simon Curtis's film *Woman in Gold* (2015), where we learn the fate of Gustav Klimt's painting *Lady in Gold* (*Dame en Or*). The painting was originally owned by and commissioned for a wealthy Jewish Viennese family, the Bloch-Bauers. Their entire family estate, including the Klimt painting, was marauded by the Nazis during the occupation. The film narrates the Bloch-Bauer saga through the painting's belated beneficiary, Maria Altmann, who was the niece of the painting's model, Adele Bloch Bauer. Maria attempts to reclaim the family painting, which in the interim had become Austrian state property, their own *Mona Lisa*. Maria's quest for ownership only reveals the impossibility of reparation to rectify history. The trial resurrects and testifies to irreparable past crimes—namely the loss of fin-de-siècle Viennese life and culture. Even though the painting is restored to Maria Altmann, it is a reminder of the impossibility of restoring "home" to the refugee or exile. Instead, the unexpected and wayward itinerary of the painting reveals how diaspora is the condition for art and life.

In chapter five, our exilic figure is inverted. In Donnersmarck's *The Lives of Others*, we see how art can undercut a totalitarian system by way of anxiety. In this case the "Other" is not the ostensible "alienated artist," but the one serving the reigning ideology that is eventually made Other by way of aesthetic experience. Despite attempts to dehumanize through state-mandated surveillance, this aesthetic experience—that is, music—puts Stasi ideology into question so that one of its most faithful adherents ends up eager to renounce it. The East German (GDR) playwright Georg Dreyman makes Gerd Wiesler anxious while he spies on behalf of the GDR by playing "Sonata for a Good Man." Moved by the music, Wiesler does not repress the anguish that the music inspires, but eventually succumbs to it and turns away (*die Wende*) from his duties of vigilant policing. Donnersmarck claimed his inspiration for the film came from a saying that Lenin couldn't listen to Beethoven's *Appassionata* as its humanizing effect might have stopped the Communist revolution. By the end of the film, music punctures Stasi ideology through the artists who unravel the alienating presence of their prurient and perverse guard. While art does not provide absolution or save citizens laboring under a totalitarian regime, *The Lives of Others* shows how it can subvert an authoritarian order.

Chapter six examines Margarethe von Trotta's *Hannah Arendt* (2012), which shows how Arendt authored a new discourse about the intellectual refugee, exile, and pariah. *Hannah Arendt* screens private details of the philosopher's life that she intentionally withheld from the public eye. The film juxtaposes Arendt's personal story with actual historic footage from the 1961 Adolf Eichmann trial to show real effects of the banality of evil. It tells how her husband, the philosopher Heinrich Blücher, helped Arendt escape from Gurs, a French internment camp, and how they both immigrated to America, living out their lives as exiles. *Arendt* illustrates and embodies what the philosopher calls a "conscious-pariah" who, like *Homo Sacer*, is the refugee or exile that inaugurates the possibility of witnessing history by way of storytelling. As both film and protagonist, *Arendt* shows how storytelling is a political act of testimony and post-Holocaust mode of invention. While not a solution to "radical evil," the film highlights the conscious pariah who works against the banality of evil to restore cultural possibility.

In chapter seven, László Nemes's *Son of Saul* (2015) shows how these films don't just depict narratives of life after death, but attempt to transform death itself. The film testifies to a mortal confrontation that makes life meaningful—that is, death as what ultimately allows for human inscription, rendering life. Saul Ausländer, a worker in the *Sonderkommando* carting bodies to the flames, tries to invent a meaningful death by burying his son, or at least a boy he claims is his son. Saul's surname, Ausländer, means "foreigner," which is emblematic of the figure exiled from human community that this book treats. Saul is Agamben's *Homo Sacer*. His wish to bury the boy's body is a way of giving himself a lineage and a death when death itself has been stolen in the camps. This act shows that even *Homo Sacer* can, by way of sacrifice, reinvent the human by making a funeral in the place of death's extermination. Likewise, Nemes's camera, which functions as a Levinasian Other, allows us to keep vigil on Saul's face, the face of the Other, the refugee, the exile, the disinherited one exterminated in the camps. The camera relentlessly follows scene after scene of the "unseen" inside the camps, *revisioning* the banality of evil.

The final chapter goes back in American Civil War history to show how imaginary aggressions like xenophobia and a fear of the Other portend authoritarian and late capital cultures. We include *The Beguiled* as a counterpoint to the Sinthomatic way of re-envisioning trauma through constructive invention since it involves exactly the opposite—namely, a sewing up and covering over of any meaningful confrontation with desire. It reflects, in our estimation, the erasure of a traumatic history rather than its constructive reinvention. Sofia Coppola's *The Beguiled* is a remake of Don Siegel's 1971 film of the same name that removes traumatic details to aestheticize Southern history. *The Beguiled* unwittingly enacts and repeats the toxic enjoyment it intends to critique by omitting traumatic details crucial for understanding the context of Southern plantation life. Slavery, incest, and black people just don't show up, despite their being key elements of the original Southern Gothic novel by Thomas Cullinan (1966). As the antipode of an uncoming community, the seminary group of women is bunkered out and settled in a former-plantation-turned-finishing-school to maintain waning aristocratic Southern values. Thus, when confronted with the wounded Irish immigrant and Union soldier named Corporal McBurney, they seduce, amputate, poison, and eventually kill him as well as the "outside" world he represents.

Revisioning War Trauma in Cinema: Uncoming Communities examines films that celebrate life in the aftermath of a traumatic past, while at the same time, critiquing the *jouissance* of our own contemporary moment. It examines films that show the real of trauma erased from history to address the ethical problems we face today. *Homo Sacer* is today's citizen-as-refugee whose commodified body is reduced to the real after being doctored, measured, surveilled, insured, sold, and exploited. More importantly, *Homo Sacer* is precisely this intimate link between citizen and refugee: a place, whether psychic or real, where we could all find ourselves. Instead of being shunned as "Other," the immigrants and war refugees revisioned in our book show us ways out of current socio-political pressures by mitigating against consensus and obedience.

The emblematic figure of uncoming communities is "the refugee [who] is perhaps the only thinkable figure for the people of our time."[29] Significantly, Agamben claims, and it is worth repeating, that this figure is possibly the "only *thinkable*" figure for "the *people*" of our time. He reminds us that thought is a pause in action; it requires reflection rather than assumption, emotion, or reaction. The pause of thought is precisely what is foreclosed when identity politics, neoliberal rhetoric, and the imaginary passions that fuel aggressive reactionary movements gaining power throughout the West take center stage. As a figure that forces a *revisioning* or rethinking of community, the refugee or exile is a paradigm for negotiating post-nationhood. As a human figure "for the people," the refugee, our contemporary *Homo Sacer*, allows the people to become people once again.

We chose to focus on the war-traumatized, refugees, and exiles because they serve as a historical mirror that reflects our own impasses—namely, and most dramatically, the Western neoliberal crisis of identity. The loss of traditions, the decline of the family, the loss of nationhood, and the new radical inequality of wealth distribution have exacerbated the imaginary demand to "belong." As a direct consequence, instances of pariahdom have multiplied. These films teach us that in the midst of this excess we are all becoming refugees. In the diaspora of uncoming communities, amidst the dissolution of the modern state, despite and even because of contemporary right-wing attempts to renew it, we see revealed what neoliberal discourse works to deny: *we are always already un-belonging.*

As a clarion call for other types of political engagement, this book focuses on traumatized war exiles and refugees in film. Instead of reducing the refugee to a scapegoat, or relating them in terms of nostalgia, these films invent via Otherness. The refugee has been the one blamed as the exception or problem, but in actuality she is the founding face and figure of invention out of crisis. In actuality, the real crisis is the end of hospitality and neighborliness—that is, shared sacrifice as a working concept for community itself. Commenting on our own historical moment, Slavoj Žižek calls the neoliberal crisis "the question that is figured in the shape of refugees, but lies in the dynamic of global capitalism."[30] Understood as such, the refugee is not the trouble with culture, but a symptom of neoliberal capitalism, citizenship, and our inability to control "borders" or divisions. This figure is an opportunity to rethink the human, rich ground for potentially revisioning the very foundation of democracy.

Revisioning War Trauma in Cinema: Uncoming Communities features films where citizens no longer seek assimilation but have accepted their pariahdom as a means for new participation. These films invent a mythic or supplemental that Hannah Arendt noted, "History [that] is no longer a closed book to them and politics . . . that focus on] refugees driven from country to country [who] represent the vanguard of their peoples."[31] This supplemental history is made through artistic invention and revisioning trauma through film. Uncoming communities originate from disaster as an opening, a point of subjective invention that rises like a phoenix out of the ashes. They extend an ethical invitation to everyone via *Homo Sacer*, which exemplifies a way of existing on the front line of aesthetic revisioning. The films invent a cinematic supplement to history that persists, echoing from the void, by witnessing the face of the Other, refugee, scapegoat, and pariah that is every citizen.

NOTES

1. Michael Witt, *Jean-Luc Godard, Cinema Historian* (Bloomington: Indiana University Press, 2013), 69.
2. See Todd McGowan, *The End of Dissatisfaction? Jacques Lacan and the Emerging Society of Enjoyment*, SUNY Series in Psychoanalysis and Culture (Albany: State University of New York Press, 2004); and McGowan, *Capitalism and Desire: The Psychic Cost of Free Markets* (New York: Columbia University Press, 2016).
3. Mari Ruti, *Between Levinas and Lacan: Self, Other, Ethics* (New York: Bloomsbury Academic, 2015), xiv, xv.
4. Cathy Caruth, *Unclaimed Experience: Trauma, Narrative, and History* (Baltimore, MD: Johns Hopkins University Press, 1996), 19.
5. Maurice Blanchot, *The Unavowable Community* (Barrytown, NY: Station Hill, 1988), 367.
6. Jacques Lacan, *On Feminine Sexuality: The Limits of Love and Knowledge*, trans. Jacques Alain Miller, vol. 20, *The Seminar of Jacques Lacan, XX* (New York: W. W. Norton, 1999), 3. Lacan defines *jouir* de as to "enjoy, take advantage of, benefit from, get off on, and so on." *Jouir* also means "to come" in the sexual sense: to reach orgasm.

7. Maurice Blanchot, *The Writing of the Disaster*, trans. Ann Smock (Lincoln: University of Nebraska Press, 1995).
8. Blanchot, *Writing of the Disaster*, 12.
9. Sigmund Freud, "Constructions in Analysis," in *The Standard Edition of the Complete Psychological Works of Sigmund Freud*, trans. James Strachey (London: Hogarth Press, 1964), 255–70.
10. Freud, "Constructions in Analysis," 262.
11. Freud, "Constructions in Analysis," 262.
12. Lacan, *Seminar: The Psychoanalytic Act*, 1967–1968.
13. Jacques Lacan, *The Sinthome: The Seminar of Jacques Lacan, Book XXIII* (Cambridge, UK: Polity, 2016).
14. Lacan, *The Sinthome*, 9.
15. Byung-Chul Han, Alain Badiou, and Erik Butler, *The Agony of Eros* (Cambridge, MA: MIT Press, 2017), 3. "Disaster" literally means "unlucky star" (*desastrum* in Latin) and functions as a moment when "catastrophic fatality abruptly switches over into salvation." It is an exposure or event like fate that both determines and opens the future.
16. Jacques Lacan, *The Four Fundamental Concepts of Psychoanalysis*, trans. Jacques-Alain Miller, *The Seminar of Jacques Lacan, XI* (New York: W. W. Norton, 1998). Lacan explains the phrase *se parer* as "*Separare*, to separate—I would point out at once the equivocation of the *se parare*, of the *se parer*, in all the fluctuating meanings it has in French. It means not only to dress oneself, but to defend oneself."
17. Blanchot, *Unavowable Community*, 10.
18. Blanchot, *Unavowable Community*, 3.
19. Blanchot, *Unavowable Community*, 11.
20. Gertrude Stein, *Everybody's Autobiography* (Boston: Exact Change, 2014), 298.
21. Walter Benjamin, "Theses on the Philosophy of History," in *Illuminations*, ed. Hannah Arendt, trans. Harry Zohn (New York: Harcourt, Brace & World, 1968), 257.
22. Benjamin, "Theses on the Philosophy of History," 257.
23. Han et al., *The Agony of Eros*, 24. Here we use *Homo Sacer* to indicate an opening beyond "bare life"; as he explains, "What is affirmed here is not bare life—which flees the negativity of death. Instead, the impulse to live, heightened to the utmost and affirmed approaches the impulse to die."
24. Giorgio Agamben, *State of Exception* (Chicago: University of Chicago Press, 2008), 3.
25. Giorgio Agamben, *Homo Sacer 1: Sovereign Power and Bare Life* (Stanford, CA: Stanford University Press, 1998), 82.
26. Agamben, *State of Exception*, 3.
27. Agamben, *State of Exception*, 28–29.
28. Claude Lanzmann, "Holocauste, la représentation impossible," *Le Monde*, March 3, 1994.
29. Agamben, *State of Exception*, 18–19.
30. Slavoj Žižek, *Refugees, Terror and Other Troubles with the Neighbors: Against the Double Blackmail* (Brooklyn, NY: Melville House, 2016), 24.
31. Hannah Arendt, "We Refugees," *Menorah Journal* 31, no. 1 (1943): 69–77.

Chapter One

Writing War Reporting Flesh *Anonyma*

A Woman in Berlin

Max Fäberböck's film *A Woman in Berlin* (2009) is an adaptation of the book *Woman in Berlin*, which was republished and translated into English in 2005.[1] The story is one woman's account of the Red Army's march into Berlin and the brutal repeated rape of German women. Choosing to remain nameless, the author publishes this text as "Anonyma," the Latin nominative feminine singular form of "anonymous." The author uses this alias to indicate agency rather than post-traumatic submission or resignation. The singular "Anonyma" denotes "one woman," a particular one, and at the same time, she is the voice of the plural. In this manner, she veils her given name, a name she had made for herself as a journalist under the Third Reich. Her evocation of anonymity is not simply a form of hiding but a particular and deliberate manner of testimony. She witnesses the destruction of symbolic law by rape and war, and comes face to face with the horror of German wartime culpability.

Woman in Berlin shows the human subject reduced to a body, to nameless flesh, forced to bear the *jouissance* of war. Anonyma makes claim to a particular form of namelessness, not as a memorial to suffering but to reveal the anonymous nature of the symbolic itself and the necessity of upholding it in the face of its destruction. Her use of the symbolic no longer relies on recognition or binaries but is an opportunity for reinvention by testifying in the place of disaster. Anonyma's account makes a different kind of history, what we have termed a sinthomatic one, that promises unimagined future possibilities through aleatory invention.

As plural, Anonyma's testimony alerts us to *other* similarly anonymous women who were unable or unwilling to speak. It stands for the thousands of

Berliners who were reduced to holes by the invading Russian army. Challenging the notion that it is not possible to speak after Auschwitz, Anonyma's testimony is a language of resistance. She writes the *Homo Sacer* raped bodies that were destined to shame and forgetting, if not to death and oblivion. In this way, *A Woman in Berlin* is paradigmatic of and figures an uncoming community. As a postwar refugee, exile, and outsider even in her own city, Anonyma is a pariah telling a truth no one wants to hear. She figures the opportunity to rethink belonging and its antithesis in a testimony that refuses naming and embraces pariahdom.

The film begins on a specific date, April 26, 1945, unlike the book, which begins five days earlier, just prior to the Red Army's invasion. Both take place during the ten days that mark the period of German surrender to the Russian Army. Each chapter starts by marking the date and time, symbolic emblems erased by the timelessness of *jouissance* of war. By writing, Anonyma keeps time, and she keeps watch, surviving together with the record she preserves. The testimony includes the time and date as a way of containing the limitlessness of trauma where one is reduced to a mound of flesh. It spans a period of eight weeks in 1945, the time period of repeated rapes by the Russian army. The book ends when Red Army troops leave the city to be stationed elsewhere. Anonyma's writing survives and sustains a testimony of the uncoming moment by constructing a future at the very instant when time is destroyed.

Anonyma was the name taken by journalist Marta Hillers, who lived to be ninety (1911–2001). Born in Germany, she studied at the Sorbonne and spoke fluent French, Russian, and German. After the Berlin occupation, she remarried and moved to Switzerland in 1950, where she lived until her death. As Anonyma, Marta Hillers uses writing and her fluency with languages, especially Russian, to preserve agency and to protect others while under siege. Here, agency and resistance are marked as linguistic, a notable distinction from the masculine agency of brute force. Moreover, her ability to speak the language of the occupiers makes Anonyma the one to whom everyone poses a demand; the women ask her for help, and the Russian army requires her to translate in order to control the population. Yet, in a biting irony, after the war, Hillers's linguistic talents did not bring her renown. Her book was blacklisted in postwar Germany. No one wanted to remember; no one wanted to hear what happened to the women of Berlin. Her account and her courage were celebrated only after her death.

The text of *Woman in Berlin* was first published in America (1954), then the same year in Geneva by Helmut Kossodo, a Jewish publisher and well-known translator who fled Germany and established himself in Switzerland. It appeared in German a few years later only to meet with immediate censure, its story discredited. As Weiden notes, in 1959 "journalist reviewers like Maria Sack questioned the authenticity of the narrator's experience and pronounced the account a false and lascivious memory of sexual relationships with members of the occupying troops."[2] In addition to these psychological reasons, early editions of Hillers's testimony were not well received. She was criticized for a narrative style that ignored social taboos when discussing sexuality. Anonyma refuses traditional notions of fear and shame in relating how the German women felt about rape and despoilment. The text reveals how by disregarding norms and deploying humor, the women were even able to laugh together and make light of the horror that befell them.

Using wit to survive the degradation and to distance themselves from their rapists, the women bypass the fate of Euripides's *Trojan Woman* and avoid becoming woefully conquered victims. Humor helps them diminish the power of their captors as well the potentially traumatic effects of the rapes. This kind of sarcasm was political, as Anja Wieden notes: "Germany's underground humor frequently referred to as whispered jokes, served as 'the mouthpiece of passive opposition.'"[3] One of the funniest scenes in the film shows the women talking about their assailants while cooking and dining. An older woman takes pride in her rapist's obscene remark about her vagina: "Ukrainian woman—like this. You—like this. The first 'like this' he illustrated with a circle formed by both his thumbs and forefingers, the second 'like this' with a single thumb and forefinger."[4] Being reduced to a body part, it seems, can even be flattering when one can make a joke of it. Anonyma shows how the women invent a female subculture that fortifies them to carry on.

Raped women were viewed as desirable, tarnished by sex, sex they supposedly "wanted." Besides the fact that blaming the victim for the shame of the Germans could not be more grossly apparent, the Freudian notion elaborated in the "Taboo of Virginity" could not be more explicit either. In Freud's essay, he explains that the woman's entire body becomes the bearer of a masculine taboo.[5] In the case of rape, women are shamed for the atrocities perpetuated by men. Such scapegoating protects the men from their own unconscious fantasies of raping and possessing women. The point is worth mentioning, since by way of such logic, the raped women are *both* the victims *and* the guilty ones. Freud himself averred, and it has been noted, that his famous discussion of "natural" feminine masochism in his essay "The Economic Problem of Masochism," was a result of his listening to male patients, not to female ones.[6] These projective mechanisms protect the very machine of fantasy, denial, and *jouissance* that animates war in the first place.

Anonyma's graphic, often journalistic depictions offended German societal norms as well as historic narratives, including postwar accounts of German shame. This is despite the fact that the Russian War monument in Berlin became known by the German women at the time as "The Tomb of the Unknown Rapist."[7] Anonyma's testimony is a "living tomb," and as such, it is a painful reminder of bodily, symbolic, and national collapse. Critics focused on historical accuracy and "actual" numbers, even though "it was impossible to determine accurately how many incidents of sexual assault the Red Army committed in the greater area of Berlin and in the eastern outskirts of the former Third Reich."[8] *Woman in Berlin* attaches a singular, reflective voice to the unknown number of plundered and nameless raped women in Berlin.

Historians have offered myriad theories to help make sense of the inordinate Russian rapes at the close of the war. They have argued that Soviet society was patriarchal, and the men were used to the idea that the spoils of war were left for the winner's taking. It has been pointed out that the Berliners' standard of living was far superior to that of their Russian invaders, whose subjugation stemmed from envy. It has also been suggested that mass rape establishes a sense of cohesion in the army, particularly in troops that have been recruited by force. The abused get to abuse someone else, someone weaker who cannot resist, and the subjugated become the subjugators, repeating their traumatic instance of military conscription.

One hypothesis is that the Russian soldiers became rapists because they were stuck in Berlin with orders to wait, and they used rape as a form of closure. What is the "end" of war? Rape is one answer to that unanswerable question. Lust replaces blood lust, and the absence of limits on what a human being can inflict on the enemy continue, only the enemy is now the *other* sex. Indeed, we might recall that for thousands of years, the army's "Other" was the woman, and rape was a last-ditch defense against castration anxiety. What does it mean that one has "won" a war, after all? Russians used rape for closure in an indefinite situation where they confronted the uncanny impotence of power. How must these men bathed in blood have felt entering the homes of civilized husbandless women, married to their enemies?

What makes *A Woman in Berlin* remarkable is not that Anonyma writes the facts of rape but the truthful, dispassionate, and direct way that she narrates them. The telling itself is an act of resistance, the speaking to the future as a nameless promise being heard. Until 2003, skepticism about the authenticity of Hillers's work and the author's identity led to heated debates about the truth-value of her testimony. The controversy over authenticity blew up after her death in 2001, when Jens Bisky, coeditor of the *Süddeutsche Zeitung*, revealed the author's name, making waves in Germany and abroad.[9] Critics called the author of *A Woman in Berlin* "crazy" and sought to silence her depiction of postwar Berlin, which contradicted "official" accounts. The projected "craziness" was her creative act, the act of giving testimony in the face of history's erasure and obliteration.

In 2003, Hans Magnus Enzensberger, an editor at *Der Spiegel*, reacted publicly to Bisky's allegations, announcing that the diary was indeed authentic, and he explained why in the forward to the book. He writes, "It is hardly remarkable that one of the best personal records of the war in Germany is a diary kept by a woman. After all it was the women who preserved an oasis of sanity in a world run amok."[10] When the book was later republished in both English and German (2005) it became a bestseller. It took two generations for Hillers's testimony to be bearable. By that time, Anonyma found not a reader, but a generation of readers. Even now, as a bestseller and feature film, the focus on controversy and historical accuracy serves to divert and distract from the work's power as a testimony of trauma and national shame.

Initially, Anonyma tells herself she is keeping this diary for her husband. It is difficult to imagine a woman in 1945 writing for someone *other* than her man. A man is the "natural" addressee for the woman, according to fascist ideology. On Saturday, April 21, 1945, at 2:00 a.m., she writes, "I'll write. It does me good, takes my mind off things. And Gerd needs to read this if he comes back—if he's still—no cross that out, mustn't jinx things."[11] The sentence is worth remarking upon because it attests to the "magical" power of everyday speech, as well as to a fundamental ambivalence present in maintaining ideals of marriage and societal ideals of belonging. Anonyma feels she might "jinx things" by imagining her husband dead; she attests to the superstitious power of thought, as though her fear that he might not return could have a power, just by saying it could come true. The act of saying, Freud points out, has a kind of power; Anonyma's crossed-out sentence attests to the power of the unconscious. It is a testament to her as a writer that she leaves in the crossed-out sentence. It is not simply that Anonyma tells the world a story it does not want to know, but language tells all of us a story we don't want to know either.

While initially writing for her husband, a Nazi at war, eventually Anonyma's narrative becomes written for a wider audience. She ends up writing for the Other as such, for the same Other that Antigone's act invokes, a universal human law greater than Creon's anxious phallic shoring up of power. The writing is a way to sustain this Other and her relation to it, thereby constructing an uncoming community. What Anonyma's narrative shows, and what she comes to learn, is that all men experience *jouissance* in a phallic way; every man resorts to it at the end of his rope—literally. As Lacan explains in his chart of sexuation, all men are related to one an*other* insofar as they are related to the exception—that is, to the father of the horde who enjoys all the women. Anonyma writes for the divided subject whose identity, like the one that Antigone supports in the face of limitless phallic power, is beyond any of its gendered incarnations. She is writing to the one for whom phallic *jouissance* is limited.

Writing is one way that Anonyma guards against oblivion. Another is her decision to "choose" her rapist and no longer be a hole for the horde. The father of the horde is certainly better than the horde. By Sunday, April 29, 1945, just days after the invasion, Anonyma ventures out in search of a soldier of higher rank. She meets Anatol, a major and a peasant, a dairy farmer from the countryside. In this moment of agency, she realizes, "For the first time I also have a sense of being a witness. There probably aren't many in this city who can talk to them [Russians]."[12] The subjective act of "choosing" her rapist is coterminous with her sense of being able to speak and to witness. Here her testimony shifts from a personal diary addressed to her husband to a Sinthomatic invention out of symbolic shards addressed to a reader.

Instead of relying on a dream of her husband's return as a source of protection, Anonyma begins to depend on writing as a form of survival. Her testimony is "the reformulating of life around the witness to death [and] to the possibility of witnessing and making history in creative acts of life."[13] Anonyma's testimony is a creative reformulation and witnessing of history by writing through trauma. It is neither nostalgic nor plaintive; it is constructive.

Such writing could only occur after a subjective change in its author. Anonyma intentionally returned to Berlin right before the Red Army invasion. In a seemingly suicidal act, she goes back to her homeland to witness its ruins. While Anonyma remains a writer, after the Russians roll in, she no longer writes like a German journalist. *A Woman in Berlin* marks a change in the nature of her reporting. It now focuses on the figure of postwar refugees and their future after the dissolution of society and nationhood. Her testimony invents something akin to our postmodern world where the notion of nation as fiction is at once powerful and principal.

What we have termed Sinthomatic writing is an undoing of meanings. Propaganda is its antithesis. Propaganda is the opposite of testimony or creative invention; it is a form not concerned with truth but, like advertising, with persuasion. Propaganda created Nazi Germany as well as the initial period of postwar Berlin. Whatever the German shame and degradation, it was nevertheless steeped in a language of bias and hate that had been used to promote a particular political ideology. It is possible to argue that Nazi propaganda prepared the way for the Red Army rapes by its coercive language and cooption of the Other. It created both the barbaric Other and the "superiority" of the one raped. Berlin was inundated by Nazi propaganda, which had been relentless in characterizing the Russians as subhuman and animalistic ("*das viehisches Treiben dieser Untermenschen*").[14] In that sense, the fascist propaganda prepared the German women to acquiesce to their "barbarous" and "philistine" Red Army occupiers.

Most Berliners accepted Joseph Goebbels's propaganda machine. Anonyma's testimony refuses to reduce the enemy to ideologically supported stereotypes, even when they seem to embody them. For example, she notes that "evidently the Russians are introducing new rationing regulations with larger allotments. . . . No so bad, if it's true. In some cases, the rations are more generous than we had lately under Adolf."[15] Here Anonyma reports that the propaganda Berliners had heard about Russians was false; the Red Army was "more generous" with rations than the Germans. Similarly, propaganda distinguished between two types of Russians—the Mongolian beast and the aristocratic gentleman. Ignoring the German rhetoric, Anonyma selects two Russians as her rapist-protectors, one from each supposed class of Russians. With both men, Anonyma engages in a seduction that refuses linguistic as well as bodily coercion, resisting the categories proffered by the current propaganda and reigning ideology.

The ability to speak the occupiers' language also puts Anonyma in the position of witnessing everyone's anger over wartime offenses, including the anger of the Russians themselves. Often, she is called on to translate Russian soldiers' renditions of Nazi crimes. In one scene, a young soldier remarks how well they treat raped German women in contrast to the way that Germans murdered Russian children. Anonyma translates this soldier's account of how the Nazis smashed the brains of Russian babies by throwing them against a wall. The soldier goes on to boast that Russian raping is not as bad as what the Germans did. Anonyma asks the soldier how he has come to know this story. He tells her he was present: "I saw it twice myself."[16]

This is a turning point in Anonyma's thinking about the war and composing her narrative as she is forced to confront the truth of the German atrocities. War atrocities don't "belong" to any particular nation; they belong to war. Now Anonyma's testimony is not limited to any one perspective, sex, race, or group but speaks for *Homo Sacer* in all forms: the enemy, the cave dweller, the rapist, the fascist, the raped woman, and even the smashed brains of the dead infants. Anonyma also writes a narrative about war rape that includes a love story.

In *Seminar XX, On Feminine Sexuality*, Lacan writes that "love is the sign . . . that one is changing discourses."[17] In this seminar, he situates love as no longer belonging to a specific discourse but as concerning the turn of his quaternary formula of the four discourses. He likens this to psychoanalysis itself. "There is something of psychoanalytic discourse when one moves from one discourse to an*other*."[18] Love, like psychoanalysis, is situated in the movement of change, as Anonyma's own experience will reveal. The accidental outcome of what happens to her with Andrei is not coerced and is unexpected. Their relationship becomes different from what Anonyma had intended with him—namely protection.

It takes all of Anonyma's linguistic and persuasive skills to seduce Andrei, the educated, cultured, powerful Major. But this seduction is not simply up to her. Initially, Anonyma decides:

> I have to find a single wolf to keep away the pack. An officer, as high-ranking as possible, a commandant, a general, whatever I can manage. After all, what

> are my brains for, my little knowledge of the enemy's language? As soon as I am able to move again [from being raped] I grab a bucket and drag myself down the stairs and out onto the street. I wander up and down . . . I practice the sentences I will use to address an officer, wondering if I don't look too green and miserable to be attractive. Physically I feel a little better, though, now that I am doing something, planning something, determined to be more than mere mute booty, a spoil of war.[19]

After being serially humiliated and violated, Anonyma decides she needs a "wolf." Ironically, she finds that the head "wolf" she has chosen turns out to be an intelligent and sensitive man. He does not consent to the role of rapist and is a man who will not give up his division even when he is in bed with her. If there is a plot to Anonyma's narrative, it is secondary to the recounting of trauma, and it concerns a change in both herself and the Russian Major. They come to have a human relationship in an inhuman world, showing how even in war the roles of enemy, victim, oppressor, and oppressed can be transformed, if only briefly.

While changing discourses concerns the *object a*, changing languages concerns identifications. It is interesting to note when characters move between Russian and German in *Eine Frau*. For the most part, the Russians use German while raping or discussing war. German is the language of assault—a language for killing. This shows that aggression is accessed in a foreign language and has to be repressed in the mother tongue. The Red Army soldiers call the women they rape "Frau Hitler"[20] to strip them of any individual identification and to make the men themselves rapists of Adolf's wife, dethroning the father's place, transgressing Oedipal boundaries. The Oedipal transgression takes place in a foreign tongue. The point is that transgression has to speak in an*other* language.

Rape tries to reduce a subject to a body and the rapist to a position of imaginary and real power: there is only the binary of the bearer and the breaker-in of the hole. While it is possible to think of rape as "the real" and, as such, outside of language, testimony invents a language that makes writing it possible. Anonyma engages in a reinvention of language to heal. Trauma surpasses the limit of speech, and Anonyma's testimony shows that rape is neither desire nor seduction. One recalls Shakespeare's "The Rape of Lucrece" in "Venus and Adonis," where he explicitly distinguishes "rape" from desire, calling Collative (the rapist's) "desire, false."[21] In this sense, Anonyma uses testimony to maintain desire through writing and does not disappear as a result.

Anonyma calls herself the Major's "whore," yet she is aware that Andrei is not really her rapist. After Anonyma visits his office and is rebuffed, Andrei comes to her partially bombed-out apartment, bringing supplies for all the inhabitants of the building. Anonyma is grateful but muses: "Am I doing it for bacon, butter, sugar, candles, canned meat? To some extent I'm sure I am." She wonders about her motives. She continues, "In addition, I like the major, and the less he wants from me as a man, the more I like him as a person. And he won't be wanting much, I can tell . . . I can actually talk with the major. Which still isn't an answer to the question of whether I should now call myself a whore, since I am essentially living off my body, trading it for something to eat."[22] Here she is questioning her own motives and noting how her desire has changed, putting her in a place she doesn't fully understand.

Both the book and film note how "war changes our words, love is no longer what it was." One is reminded of George Steiner's reflection in *Language and Silence* that words will never mean anything after "the world of Auschwitz [which] lies outside speech as it lies outside reason."[23] Anonyma shows that language can be resuscitated precisely because it doesn't fully mean what you think it does and because it carries in it the possibility for non-understanding. *A Woman in Berlin* shows that war throws into question the meaning not only of nationhood but also of basic symbolic signifiers such as identity, love, enemy, ally, or bad. She muses, "What is that supposed to mean, anyway—a bad person?"[24] In war the meaning of words changes due to the erasure or shifting of discourse.

Eventually Andrei gets annoyed with the fact that her *other* lover/protector, Anatole, the soldier/dairy farmer, continues to visit. Andrei asks Anonyma if they can be exclusive by giving her a bicycle. He asks her, "What's better, my bike or his cock?"[25] Just as Andrei had refused to rape Anonyma when she gave him the opportunity and instead brought food, he offers her the bike as distinct from the organ. This offer presents her with a choice to either stay on the side of *jouissance*, with Anatole, or to be in the world of culture, able to move about more freely. Moreover, the question allows her to wonder about her own *jouissance* in her desire for "protection." Anonyma chooses the bike, and she rides it through the remainder of the film. The beautiful bike scenes show Anonyma's mobility as she cycles fast, sailing through the bombed-out city. She cycles like she writes—dashing about deftly, able to avoid becoming part of the rubble.

After she accepts the bike, Andrei installs his men to guard and protect Anonyma from being raped. In an exemplary scene of Andrei's protection, we witness how his love for her directly conflicts with his position as Major. A young German man in Anonyma's apartment building kills a Russian officer whom he caught raping his girlfriend. Under the occupation, Germans were forbidden to possess weapons, and this young man, protecting his girlfriend, evidently had hidden a weapon. Despite the military edict, only the guilty young man is killed, and Andrei saves Anonyma as well as everyone in her building. Andrei fights with an officer of lower rank who wants to raze the structure to the ground and kill everyone in it as revenge. The point is that the relation between Anonyma and Andrei necessitates a change in regard to the laws that previously formed them.

Contrary to what she was taught by German propaganda, Anonyma notes that unlike German men, Russian men actually appreciate educated women. Indeed, we see many of the characters fatigued by misinformation and hackneyed oppositional rhetoric. Somehow aware of how they've been influenced, Andrei and Anonyma are careful when they speak together of politics. For example, when Andrei asks Anonyma, "What is fascism?" she replies, "The word comes from the Roman 'bundle of reeds.'"[26] Her response is a refusal to engage in clichéd ideology and underlines etymology instead. With Andrei, Anonyma uses language not only to translate or communicate, but also to seduce and play. She refers to Russian literature and Pushkin's summer residence, which impresses him.

The film also includes a minor character, a female Russian soldier named Masha.[27] Conscripted female combatants in the Red Army witnessed the Berlin rapes and did not protest. This fact shows how the military can make men even out of women. Masha's desire and desirability are erased and absorbed by military group thinking and ideals of belonging. She is in love with the Major and warns Anonyma to "keep her hands off Andrei." Masha says this to Anonyma in a fit of jealous anger, adding, "He will never love you because the Germans killed his wife!" Andrei is not interested in the younger Masha, who is unable to think critically about the enemy or even consider some of her own comrades as human. She insults a Mongolian soldier who guards Anonyma, claiming he is lower class in an attempt to retrench her power through bullying and racism.

Contrarily, Anonyma's writing compels us to rethink identifications, especially group-think regarding the enemy. *Woman in Berlin* affirms the feminine singular over sameness, belonging, and consensus. In *Group Psychology and the Analysis of the Ego*, Freud mentions how "it is a pleasurable experience for those who are concerned to surrender themselves so unreservedly to their passions and thus to become merged in the group and to lose the sense of the limits of their individuality."[28] Group bonding stemming from passion rather than rational thought was a feature of both sides; it is a feature that constructs a "side." Anonyma's entire testimony challenges this type of bonding and the "pleasurable experience" of surrender to the group. In the act of writing, she refuses to surrender to any group, including her countrymen, the "victimized" women, or the brutal Russian invaders.

At the end of the film, the Major asks Anonyma to call him Andrei, marking a level of intimacy that is abruptly interrupted when he is immediately transferred. Hearing a rumor that he is leaving Berlin, Anonyma rushes to him on the bike he gave her to say goodbye. He has been restationed and departs without letting her know, lending credence to perhaps the film's motto: "War changes our words, love is no longer what it was." His symbolic position once again requires that Major Andrei remain with his men. This occurs while Anonyma's husband Gerd returns home from war but leaves abruptly after reading her journals and destroying their former apartment. Importantly, it is her German husband who destroys her apartment, not her Russian rapists. This action as well as the departure of Andrei reveals not only a change in Anonyma and the Major but in the fate of the city itself. It indicates Berlin as one face of the uncoming community, a place where symbolic markers of identity become ambiguous, if not moot.

One recalls the images of bombed-out Berlin filmed on location in Rossellini's classic *Germany Year Zero* (1948),[29] the title of which connotes a timeless world with no future—where sons kill fathers, teachers abuse children, and children commit suicide. *Germany Year Zero* was filmed in 1947, with actual scenes shot in the ruins of postwar Berlin. Rossellini shot amidst the rubble and recruited war survivors for actors. He took traumatized citizens off the streets and into his camera, giving them new life. Rossellini ends his film where *Woman in Berlin* begins: with the woman. In the Italian classic, a woman stands in despair over the body of a child who committed suicide. Both films portray Berlin as a city without law; there are no German men left; there is no future and no possibility of transmission except through the films themselves.

While Billy Wilder's classic, *A Foreign Affair* (1948),[30] also highlights the role of women in Berlin's postwar rubble, it nevertheless buttresses many of the traditional ideals that Rossellini and Marta Hillers work to critique. The Dietrich character plays a glorified whore, who is unlike Anonyma since she is in control and not threatened by rape. Dietrich's character directs her own path and is the partner to the man in power, whether he is a Nazi or an American. The wily, shrewd, highly sexual, worldly wise woman is contrasted with the uptight, moral congresswoman, comically named "Miss Frost," played by Jean Arthur. This congresswoman perversely seeks out all the decadence of the Dietrich nightclub singer, denouncing her, only to fall in love herself with Dietrich's lover, the American colonel. America and Berlin cross when Dietrich's Berlin nightclub singing meets a cheerleading "Io-way!" the ballad of the Midwest state. When Colonel Johnny finds himself caught between the two women, he protects the naive Miss Frost. At the end of the film, Johnny is being chased by Miss Frost, who will "get her man," but this "getting," now a moral one, is one that a postwar American audience can "get behind." Wilder's *A Foreign Affair* romanticizes America and resuscitates imaginary notions of marriage, purity, and belonging that prefigure, albeit perhaps unwittingly, the social norms of the fifties. This is the antithesis of the uncoming communities created in *Woman in Berlin* and *Germany Year Zero*, which invent out of the shards of history to film.

After World War II, Berlin was "liberated" (*Befreiung*) by the Russian army and occupied and partitioned by the Americans, the Russians, and the

English. It was no longer a German city. The Germans described this liberation as a "collapse" (*Zusammenbruch*). Citizens could no longer identify and rely on nationhood, or Germanness. Berlin became a city divided where social unity dissolved. *Woman in Berlin* shows the ersatz nature of belonging and how citizens of Berlin were changed by the collapse of Nazi Germany. Anonyma describes Berlin as a city of cave dwellers or citizens condemned to the diaspora. Even today, Berlin, like New York City, is full of people with no common group identity. This lack of group identity is fertile ground for an uncoming community that makes neighbors out of loss, specifically the loss of imaginary belonging.

The films in this book include postwar Berlin as a site of the uncoming community, a space for invention amidst disaster, rape, and anarchy. Other films in this collection that are set in Berlin include Florian Henckel von Donnersmarck's *The Lives of Others*,[31] where the artist/playwright ironically influences an officer who is surveilling him, and Nellie in Christian Petzold's *Phoenix*,[32] also played by the actress Nina Hoss. In *Phoenix*, Nelly is a concentration camp survivor who returns home to Berlin to find only betrayal. The city is a site for Sinthomatic invention that transforms a traumatic past through aesthetic engagement instead of fetishizing or objectifying it in history.

Anonyma describes Berlin as "a city of abandoned gardens." This description is true—nature is no longer tended to or cultivated—but it is also a metaphor for the feminine, for nature brought to civilization, the garden. Berlin is a city of abandoned women, the soon-to-be-damaged gardens. She writes, "The war is rolling towards Berlin . . . now and then whole hours pass in eerie silence. Then all of a sudden you remember that it's spring. Clouds of lilac perfume drift over from untended gardens and waft through the charred ruins of apartment houses."[33] Here lilac signals the smell of both decay and beauty wafting over the city, like the famous association in *Double Indemnity* between the smell of honeysuckle and murder.[34] Given what follows it is impossible not to see the ruined city as one big whorehouse, a "whoredom" which is a projection of both Red Army and Nazi masculinist ideology.

Anonyma compares Berlin to Dostoevsky's underground as an opposing space or sequestered place that critiques and underlines the impossibility of community itself. In her own "notes from the underground," Anonyma writes, "The Russians have the streets entirely to themselves. But under every building people are whispering, lurking. Who could ever imagine such a whole other world hidden here, so frightened, right in the middle of the big city. Life sequestered underground and split into tiny cells so that no one knows what anyone else is doing."[35] Berliners are forced below, unable to emerge above or move about freely. Storming the city isn't enough; the

Russians penetrate the underground cells looking for women. They occupy the city down to its bowels.

In postwar Berlin, nothing was off-limits; all flesh, even bodies dear to us, could be consumed. This is underlined in *Woman in Berlin* by the repeated shot of the roaming stray dog in the city wreckage. This shot is a citation, seen originally in Kurosawa's *Yojimbo* (1961),[36] where the city was overrun by villains. The shot is used again in Nikita Mikhalkov's *12* (2007),[37] showing a Chechen village destroyed by Russian invaders. The stray dog with a human hand in its jaw shows not only that it is a dog-eat-dog world but that Berlin has become a city where people are reduced to dogs that eat their neighbors. It has become a traumatic space without taboos, an *umwelt* of consumption. The film shows the city as an animal kingdom, as Lacan notes: "For animals, neither rapes, nor all of those complications, all the fuss we make over it ever appear."[38] In this anarchic place, human hands no longer make the world by handshakes but are consumed. *Woman in Berlin* ends with a child asking, "Mutti, can we eat the horse?"[39] The horse in question is the family's own trusted animal. The kingdom of flesh has overturned the rule of law.

It is tempting to compare the rubble of Berlin to the rubble of our democracy today, which has crumbled beneath the blitz of bullying and media propaganda. Juliet MacCannell wrote presciently of this in the Clinton era when she remarked how girls growing up now experience an inordinate amount of "obscenity that [literally] has landed . . . in the girl's lap."[40] She underlines that we live in an era that is not only full of media obscenity but also something real, "the unspeakable horrors to which we are daily exposed, to which we are growing increasingly numb."[41] MacCannell's critique foreshadowed our own moment. Russian cyber-propaganda, troll farms, new algorithmic techniques to aid the spread of disinformation, and media manipulation of U.S. opinion pervades our newsfeeds and screens. The obscene is no longer hidden. In the famous *Access Hollywood* tape, now president Trump displays a casual attitude toward assault on a woman: "I moved on her like a bitch. She was married so I couldn't get there but I tried."[42] The animal kingdom is right here. Trump's claim to "move on her" is a military metaphor of invasion or of animal behavior toward "the bitch." The state of the social tie is such that Trump was not vilified for this statement, and it may have even helped him get elected. In group *jouissance*, as sustained by Fox and Breitbart, violent sexual and racial passions rule. There is no more invitation, dialogue, or play, only assault.

Woman in Berlin challenges us to avoid propping up the imaginary in response to the dissolution of social ties. Instead, Anonyma's courage inspires Sinthomatic invention as an antidote to both disinformation *and* information culture, our blitz-bullying media today. *Woman in Berlin* uses testimony to present, contain, and delimit *jouissance*. Her work challenges propaganda by providing a particular account of disaster. Anonyma's testimony is a singular voice that speaks for a multitude critiquing supposed primary narratives to construct an account of trauma, a writing of *jouissance*.

NOTES

1. Anonymous, *A Woman in Berlin: Eight Weeks in the Conquered City: A Diary*, trans. Philip Boehm and Marta Hillers (New York: Picador/Henry Holt, 2006); Max Färberböck, dir., *The Downfall of Berlin: Anonyma* (Strand, 2008).
2. Anja Wieden, "Writing Resistance: Anonyma's Narration of Rape in *A Woman in Berlin*," *Women in German Yearbook: Feminist Studies in German Literature & Culture* 32 (2016): 34.
3. Wieden, "Writing Resistance," 36.
4. Anonymous, *A Woman in Berlin*, 127.
5. Sigmund Freud, "The Taboo of Virginity," in *Standard Edition of the Complete Psychological Works of Sigmund Freud*, vol. 11 (London: Hogarth Press, 1957), 193–218.
6. Sigmund Freud, "The Economic Problem of Masochism," in *Collected Papers*, ed. James Strachey, vol. 5 (London: The Hogarth Press, 1950), 255–68.
7. Lucy Ash, "The Rape of Berlin," *BBC News*, May 1, 2015, sec. Magazine, http://www.bbc.com/news/magazine-32529679.
8. Wieden, "Writing Resistance," 32.
9. Weiden, "Writing Resistance," 27.
10. Anonymous, *A Woman in Berlin*, xii.
11. Anonymous, *A Woman in Berlin*, 11.
12. Anonymous, *A Woman in Berlin*, 78.
13. Cathy Caruth, *Literature in the Ashes of History* (Baltimore: Johns Hopkins University Press, 2013), 5.
14. Atina Grossman, "A Question of Silence: The Rape of German Women by Occupation Soldiers," *October* 72 (1995): 50.
15. Anonymous, *A Woman in Berlin*, 177.
16. Anonymous, *A Woman in Berlin*, 133.
17. Jacques Lacan, *On Feminine Sexuality: The Limits of Love and Knowledge*, trans. Jacques Alain Miller, vol. 20, *The Seminar of Jacques Lacan, XX* (New York: W. W. Norton, 1999), 16.
18. Lacan, *On Feminine Sexuality*, 21.
19. Anonymous, *A Woman in Berlin*, 64.
20. Max Färberböck, *The Downfall of Berlin*.
21. William Shakespeare and John Roe, *The Poems: Venus and Adonis, the Rape of Lucrece, the Phoenix and the Turtle, the Passionate Pilgrim, A Lover's Complaint: Updated Edition* (Cambridge: Cambridge University Press, 2012).
22. Anonymous, *A Woman in Berlin*, 116.
23. George Steiner, *Language and Silence: Essays on Language, Literature, and the Inhuman* (New York: Atheneum, 1967), 123.
24. Anonymous, *A Woman in Berlin*, 117.
25. Anonymous, *A Woman in Berlin*, 141.
26. Anonymous, 99.
27. See Färberböck, *Downfall of Berlin*. Masha is played by Aleksandra Kulikova.
28. Sigmund Freud, *Group Psychology and the Analysis of the Ego*, trans. Ethel Spector Person (Hillsdale, NJ: Analytic Press, 2001), 23.
29. Roberto Rossellini, dir., *Germany Year Zero* (Criterion, 1948).
30. Billy Wilder, dir., *A Foreign Affair* (Paramount, 1948).
31. Florian Henckel von Donnersmarck, dir., *The Lives of Others*, 2007.
32. Christian Petzold, dir., *Phoenix*, 2014.
33. Anonymous, *A Woman in Berlin*, 1.

34. Billy Wilder, dir., *Double Indemnity*, 1944.
35. Anomymous, *A Woman in Berlin*, 46.
36. Akira Kurosawa, dir., *Yojimbo*, 1961.
37. Nikita Mikhalkov, *12*, Crime, Drama, Thriller, 2007.
38. Jacques Lacan, "On Psychoanalytic Discourse," trans. Jack Stone, *La Salmanara*, 1978, 32–55.
39. Anonymous, *A Woman in Berlin*, 261.
40. Juliet Flower MacCannell, *The Hysteric's Guide to the Future Female Subject* (Minneapolis: University of Minnesota Press, 2000), 33.
41. MacCannell, *Hysteric*, 33.
42. David Fahrenthold, "Trump Recorded Having Extremely Lewd Conversation about Women in 2005," *Washington Post*, October 8, 2016, https://www.washingtonpost.com/politics/trump-recorded-having-extremely-lewd-conversation-about-women-in-2005/2016/10/07/3b9ce776-8cb4-11e6-bf8a-3d26847eeed4_story.html.

Chapter Two

Belonging Is Uncanny

Wakolda, *or* The German Doctor

The German Doctor, both[1] as novel and film,[2] serves as a critique of the imaginary: of ideals and ideology, and most importantly, of the fantasy of belonging. It demonstrates the *unheimlich* confrontation between a neurotic wish for phallic being and a psychotic certitude, incarnated here as the Nazi imaginary. The certitude that had such cultural power as legitimate, as an officially sanctioned *weltanschauung*, was already shown to be waning at the historical moment at which the novel is situated. The story takes place *after* the war—after this fantasy of belonging or of "taking one's proper, fated place" was exposed to the world with all the unprecedented criminal horror it authorized. It was not simply the souls and the minds of people that were implicated by this totalizing ideology, but the Real of the body, which was experimented upon and supposedly "bettered," was reduced to real matter—matter to be changed, "ameliorated," and even discarded.

The German Doctor is a film directed by Lucia Puenzo and adapted from her own semi-fictional novel, *Wakolda*, about Josef Mengele's encounter with a family in postwar Argentina. After ingratiating himself to their adolescent daughter Lilith, Mengele also begins experimenting on her mother Eva, who is pregnant with twins. Even though Lilith's father, Enzo, expressly forbids Dr. Mengele's experiments, the women decide to participate in secret.

The paternal function is rendered powerless at a juncture where a neurotic wish meets up with a psychotic answer. The film poignantly underscores the powerlessness of paternal doubt when confronted with the certainty of the doctor's Real response, a failure implicated in the rise of fascist ideology itself. The wish is made all the more present in the film in the young protagonist's life by way of maternal demand from which she is barely separated. Who would possibly say no, after all, to finally and really belonging?

The historic setting of the film allows us to revision our current ideological challenges. The persistence of the vitality of fallacious Nazi "science" after the war is used to illuminate our contemporary moment in which subjectivity is jettisoned in favor of the satisfactions of an ideology that supports and sustains narcissism. We are enjoined daily to belong to an imaginary set of standards and demands and to sacrifice our better judgment. Set in Argentina after the war, "home" to the fled Nazis, it is in the Nazi Diaspora that we become all the more acutely aware of the uncanny nature of the drive to belong. In the story, the Nazi push to perfection confronts the wishes of a twelve-year-old girl, on the brink of becoming a woman. The encounter betrays our own secret wishes in our post-capitalist moment wherein femininity is ensnared at the imaginary and real level to support phallic hegemonic ideology. Due to technology, the Real female body can be used nowadays in ways heretofore unthinkable. In this regard, it is significant that the main protagonists are named Eva and Lilith. The reference to Genesis emphasizes that what is at stake is a lost paradise—a place where we (not just Nazis, but all of humanity) are presumed to have once "belonged." To find one's proper place, then, is the promise of paradise.

The fact that the story's protagonist is named Lilith, and her mother is Eva, calls attention to the difference between the maternal and the feminine, further underscoring this original "Edenic" loss. According to Lacan, the woman is "not-all" as distinct from the mother, who, insofar as she is a mother, is always in a fundamentally phallic position. Lilith was *not* an actual biblical figure but one presumed to have existed by apocryphal Rabbinic interpretation, according to which she was the first "Woman." Supposedly ousted from God's original creation, scratched for Eve, Lilith is invented to explain the double invention of woman in the two Genesis stories. In the first story, she is not named. Lilith is thus imagined as the scrapped woman, as though God made a mistake when creating woman and had to do it over again to get it right. Lilith, therefore, does "not exist"; she never "existed"—to parody Lacan's thesis about Woman, her name in Hebrew comes from the word "night." Our Lilith—the protagonist of the film/novel (*The German Doctor/Wakolda*)—is twelve years old and concerned, as is her mother, by the fact that she is the shortest girl in her class. A foreign, handsome stranger—a doctor—will promise her not only growth but great height, which he tells her she was destined for. Such a promise of narcissistic phallic restoration is comparable to those proffered in our contemporary world to women by industry and medicine, and not only by surgically enhancing, but nowadays by genetically producing a more "desirable" outcome. In this sense, "Lilith" is a woman precisely insofar as she has "never existed" and "falls short" of the imaginary standard of what "woman" is supposed to be.

The film opens with a family traveling to Lilith's mother Eva's first home in the heart of Patagonia following the end of World War II. Little do they suspect that this journey threatens a real "return" that concerns not simply an imaginary wish, but an encounter with a doctor escaped from Auschwitz living under a false name who will promise that such a "return" to the German language as well as to idealized physical perfection is possible. This mysterious stranger posing as a bookish veterinarian is full of secrets. He was the one who ran a famous medical laboratory and was known as "God" in Auschwitz and Birkenau, who in the name of bettering the race for the good of the Reich had absolute power over the life and death of his subjects.[3] He was the one whose "passion for research made him totally blind to the misery of the camp," whose "commitment to the principle of murder-selection was inexorable"; in short, he was one for whom the return to paradise was no dream.[4]

The film is called *Wakolda*, named after Lilith's childhood doll. It was renamed *The German Doctor* for American audiences, playing on America's fear and hate of Nazis, hoping to boost ticket sales. The altered film title, alluding of course to Mengele without naming him, only underscores what Jay Lifton in his book *The Nazi Doctors* claims about the infamous "monster"—namely, that "no war criminal has evoked so much fantasy and fiction."[5] Not "naming" the doctor only gives him more imaginary power by way of suggestion and produces anxiety: Is he *the* doctor? Our own excited and prurient curiosity should give us pause as we wonder what precisely we are trying to discover via naming him.

Wakolda, the original name of the novel and the film (as it appeared outside the United States), means "Mapuche" or "Mapuche doll" in Spanish.[6] Not a name that evokes drama or intrigue for the North American audience, the Mapuche were a group of indigenous Indians inhabiting southwestern Argentina, including parts of present-day Patagonia, an area devastated by the Spanish conquistadors years ago and subsequently again by colonization. The doll is described in the novel as having "long black hair, down to her knees. Her face, hands and feet were carved from wood, and she had gigantic black eyes. Her nose was straight and her lips were thick and she had a swollen belly and wore a hand-woven tunic."[7] This doll is a "native," a non-ideal doll, her thick lips and swollen belly exaggerating her reproductive traits like the ancient Stone Age Venus figures. The doll used in the film, however, is not Mapuche but a fair blonde doll with blue eyes, like the film's blonde protagonist, Lilith. The difference in title and in the figure of the doll between the film and the book is worth considering. The film, with a more global mass market appeal in mind, had to make the doll blonde. The Mapuche doll could not be loved or as easily identified with by a film-going audience for whom loving a doll is impossible unless it is a blonde and blue-eyed one—a girl, rather than a sexualized dark-skinned woman. Perhaps we might wonder about the role America has in exporting and promoting imaginary ideals of belonging, and the power of American Girl, a doll whose sales have even surpassed Barbie globally for the past several years.[8] Girls are more phallic than women since, unlike women, they do not lack; they are still phallic for their mothers who are intimately invested in them, and they, in turn, in their mothers' investment. While not twins, this mother-daughter passion is nevertheless another mirror that the German doctor seeks to restore to them by way of his "cure."

The story circulates around the exchange of this doll between the doctor and Lilith, the protagonist and the film's narrator. Her narrative voice becomes her response to "being the doll" as an assumed feminine destiny—although we could think of the fate differently in the film and the novel. In the novel, the sexualized, native Wakolda doll is Lilith's love object, one that differs from her but one to which she is attached. She has to separate herself from the doctor and his aims in order to care for that doll *as lost*. In the film, however, it is the doll as the idealized narcissistic object that she must separate from; in either case, it is Lilith who must learn to doubt her own wish. She will be able to do so with the help of another woman—the school librarian and photographer archivist, Nora Eldoc. Eventually, by way of her narrative, Lilith subjectifies an encounter with a traumatic potential plenitude, where a neurotic wish and a maternal demand are potentially fulfilled by a psychotic "who knows." Her art, namely the novel and the film, is to be distinguished from the imaginary perfection promised by the doll and the restoration of the mirror relation between mother and daughter. The doctor promises an acephalic infinity, depicted in the film as the mass, factory-produced doll he offers to finance. Lilith's beloved doll was handmade individually by her father Enzo, an artisan who makes dolls in his spare time, and who, importantly, unlike the mother and Lilith, does not speak German. The German doctor is "superior" to the artisan father at first glance; he is more handsome, more elegant, worldlier—and he is wealthy. He can improve the doll by making it in great quantities, and as an all-powerful doctor, he can even improve on the father's creations—his daughter and his twins—correcting human beings' "defects."

The ethics of the film concern the giving up of such imaginary quests. Instead of achieving Mengele's promised end—either in terms of Lilith's hoped-for growth spurt or of the establishment of a booming doll manufacturing company—Lilith tells her story. She leaves a testimony of her encounter at the age of twelve with "an omnipotent rescuer and concerned physician," one wholly dedicated to the "noble goal" of "advancing the search to unlock the secret of multiplying the race of superior beings destined to rule."[9] To leave a testimony is the only way to grow up, and it does not concern her size.

As the film's title and as Lilith's favorite doll, *Wakolda* suggests that belonging necessarily concerns nostalgia, one that evokes the wishes of childhood. *Wakolda*, like the indigenous Mapuche Indians who were cast out, shows the impossibility of feeling fully at home or restored after becoming an exile in one's own homeland—whether as an indigenous people to a land or as a young adolescent to a body. Real changes in the body occur during puberty. One is ousted from one's own bodily "home" as one develops adult secondary sexual characteristics. The German doctor's promise of belonging would "restore" the place and the body of Lilith and, by analogy, of the Wakolda doll, a symbol of restoring an entire people to its birthplace, and even to the idea that a birthplace is a proper place. It is the false promise that the Mapuche would finally belong to their birthplace—or that anyone would ever finally "belong," as a destiny, anywhere. It is a false promise that Lilith is destined to her phallic place and body, as though the lack that marks the feminine body and the desire it arouses could finally find a phallic solution; as though the puberty that Lilith was beginning to experience as a separation from her mother would be remediated and mother and daughter would be united again in their maternal *unheimlich* homeland; as though the German people would finally take their rightful destined place in the world order; as though American Girl would finally be the best-selling doll in the world . . . and it is!

Mengele meets Lilith after she *drops* her doll. He sees the doll fall and picks it up for her. The "dropping of the doll" is an overdetermined metaphor: for puberty, for becoming a woman, for relinquishing the phallic place she held for her mother. A fall sets up the drama of the film, namely the relation of the doll to an imaginary ideal that Lilith (literally) falls short of, one that Mengele promises to restore and that Lilith's mother desires for her: "normalcy" above all. Here, Lilith's growth into womanhood is only considered as real—*not* as subjective. Mengele is in the position of restoring the imaginary phallus to the Other, to the "health of the master race," and his particular madness encounters a wish of mother and daughter: of restoring Lilith as phallic to her mother and to her mother's dream for her daughter and thus for herself. His power over them is obvious; they are both fascinated by him and intuitively know to keep their relation with him a secret from the father.

The doctor's slightly erotically tinged looks at the young Lilith are as intense as they are ambiguous. Lilith, like the many children Mengele experimented upon, thinks she is loved by him, only to discover that his passion pertains only to his own mad vision, one that has nothing to do with her except as a "scientific" specimen for furthering his "research." In such a promised paradisaical restoration, the doll would never be lost. In fact, there would have never been a human being to begin with, only raw material for the making of the ideal. Nothing would ever have to fall; nothing need be lost. Do we not sense something of the promises of Botox, plastic surgery, juice fasts, enforced exercise, and the "paradise" of late capital? If paradise is restored we will never have to age.

For Freud, neurotic anxiety concerns a fall, a *Niederkommen*, which gives birth to lack. In the film, this lack is *literally* sutured by the doctor, who sees such work as his great mission. In this sense, he fulfills the promise of the imaginary plenitude that Nazi ideology sought to ensure. Illustrating this fact is a short scene in which a dog bites off the doll's leg and the doctor stitches it back on. While stitching up the doll, the doctor "knew immediately that he had found a solution for his nostalgia. It was of no importance that the baby was porcelain. He could do what he wanted with it without raising anyone's suspicions. Lilith held her breath, her attention fixed on the dance of the needle as it wove in and out of the bandage, seeking out the holes made by the teeth and joining the foot to the rest of the body."[10]

We are reminded of Hoffmann's doll and the evil Coppelius who had power over its dismemberment, as he "bleated" over the famous "mechanism of the hands and the feet,"[11] not to mention the eyes. While Dr. Mengele sought the restoration as the "solution" to his "nostalgia," we note in this excerpt that Lilith sought out the holes, aiming at the lack or the maiming itself rather than its repair. For Mengele, Lilith herself is a doll to be repaired, making him all the more the "evil twin" of the father of the Freudian uncanny. Josef Mengele was even called "Father" in the camp due to the air of authority he exuded, especially as the absolute master of the selections on the ramp, which earned him the title "The Angel of Death." The ultimate doctor of the final solution, known for his "absolute ideological firmness," Mengele was always restoring the imaginary plenitude of the Other, suturing all lack in the name of the ideal. The German doctor imagines himself able to cure life itself. It is no wonder then that he was a murderer on such a grand scale, since the only real cure for life is death.

The position of Mengele in the camps was that of a god. This was promulgated by his presiding over the selections and the sense, even from people close to him, that "nobody ever really understood what he wanted."[12] This enigmatic quality made him even more mysterious; people spoke of the principle of "unfathomability" that surrounded him.[13] He was even reputed to have had "no sense for women," despite the fact that many prisoners compared him to a "Hollywood actor," and even to Rudolph Valentino, further adding to his position of being unaffected and beyond desire.[14] One inmate said of the real Mengele: "He always carried an aura with him of some terrifying threat. . . . I have found it nearly impossible to transmit the edge of this terror."[15] One prisoner doctor put it simply: "He wanted to be God—to create a new race."[16] In the novel, in Argentina, the doctor can only enact his magic while hiding and in secret. He is already less powerful, having been made so by the judgment of the world.

The distinction between the normal and the pathological is a major theme of the film, underlining their uncanny infection of one another as it becomes impossible to isolate either. What Lifton calls the "healing-killing paradox" that epitomized the overall function of the Nazi regime is just one of the many uncanny paradoxes that we see in the unfolding of the story. Such impossible dualities abound, including some particular to Mengele himself, notably a strange combination of "affection and violence," as well as a strange mélange of disaffected superiority coupled with an excited passion for "research." In the "medical" journal he keeps of Lilith's "progress," the doctor notes the first signs of pubescence as though he were noting an aberrancy. Mengele aims to "treat Lilith's 'dysmorphia,'" yet being short is hardly dysmorphia. The historic Mengele was known to have drawn a line at 5'–5'2" in the children's *Lager* and to have told them that they had to reach that height or they would be selected.[17] He was also known to have collected dwarfs among his twins[18] and to have "relished" his dwarfs "ecstatically."[19] Being short for her age, Lilith inspires the doctor's passion to "cure," always imbricated in his equally ardent passion to kill.

We further glean the bizarre nature of the doctor's medical interventions in his criticism of Eva when he indicates her pregnancy with twins is in jeopardy and she requires his medical intervention. The guiding idea behind his "medicine" or what was known was the Nazi biomedical vision—where he studied twins for genetics—as well as Mengele's passionate personal commitment to bringing science to the Nazi vision is, in our view, the attempt to stabilize the mirror. In the film, he promises to make the twins equal in size and strength. This passion for sameness was also alive and well in Mengele's notorious fascination with heterochromia, a condition where one eye differs in color from the second. He was known to extract and collect eyes from such subjects, enthralled as he was by this anomaly. Similarly, his well-known obsession with twins, a passion he will remain notorious for in perpetuity, was the logical outcome of Nazi ideology, since if a mirror could finally exist without a stain—without any difference or lack—the promise of imaginary perfection could finally be achieved, and the first alienation that would portend human subjective postlapsarian existence would be rendered null and void; we would never have to leave the valley of the dolls.

Mengele constantly creates a series of doubles in an attempt to give meaning to his life's work, a paean to the "mirror in perpetuity": with Lilith and her doll, with her father's dolls, with the twins, and even with the farm animals. Yet no matter what he is working on, Mengele is always doing the same work—that is, trying to construct a stable, faultless mirror. Nazi ideology is a paranoiac; an ideal ego rules, and anything less than ideal is duly exterminated. Hence, Lilith and Eva—*like all women*—are in the position of always being the "not big enough" or "right enough" ego—especially if we consider the feminine in Lacanian terms as that which cannot be signified but concerns a hole in the structure. Mengele sees himself as "doctor" to this imperfect ego, that is, this nascent feminine, one on the brink of puberty, which is—*and only is*—himself. Or, we could posit that the passion that fuels his work is a way of staving off the push to the woman, and that is why his passion is so totalizing. After meeting Mengele, Lilith narrates: "The first time he met me, he thought I was the perfect specimen." Already she is reduced in his eyes to a "specimen," a scientific experiment, meeting with every girl's desire to be something Real for someone, although she could not know how. His proposed "cure" for the deficient feminine Real is an imaginary bereft of any symbolic anchor. We see this structure as psychotic in his attempt to fill and sustain the whole of the mother and to avoid the feminine via the phallic nature of the child.

The tropes of doubling, the mirror, the doll, and even the narrator as having her vision intact (like Hoffmann's Klara) continually mark the disturbing and anxious world of the Hoffmannesque uncanny. In this unstable world, the doll is shared by the neurotic and the psychotic; the difference, however, is that for the neurotic, the object falls; for the psychotic it must be sustained infinitely since there is no separation, no *Niederkommen*, no fall possible. In psychosis, the subject and the object are sutured, or as Lacan says, the psychotic "has the object in his pocket."[20] Mengele's work aims at imaginary perfection, which can never be fulfilled in its aspirational exceptionality since the very possibility of that exceptionality is destroyed by the fact that the ideal requires the work of infinite doubling. The "final solution" of the perfect mirror has to be repeated infinitely and, as such, can never be final or a solution at all.

Mengele compares himself to an artist, yet he admits to preferring weighing and measuring to creating. When Lilith asks him what he keeps in his journal, he asserts that poets write about what they see, painters paint; but he measures and weighs what interests him. Mengele avers that he is not making art. But what is he doing? It is a strange kind of knowing—measuring and weighing—as though the Other could be summed up, reduced to its size and weight, reduced to a Real materiality with no remainder. The historic Mengele was notorious for weighing and measuring everyone to the very last detail; it was a fact attested to by all the survivors of his medical experiments. This passion was so great, it even caused his fellow Auschwitz doctors to comment after the war that Mengele seemed to have become "lost in the details" to the point where he "detoured from the aims of science." It is as though weighing and measuring became, in themselves, his greatest enjoyment. Don't we see in this activity the very aim of Nazi ideology? What else is there to do but reduce a person to her parts and reduce those parts to inventory, to raw material that can be categorized, filed away, and stored.

In the film, we get to peek at his journals, where he reveals himself in strange, uncanny "medical" sketches, which are neither art nor medicine but a bizarre mix of both, and which belong to a logic entirely his own. His "scientific observational sketches" of Eva, Lilith, and the twins are more "real" to him than the actual people he encounters. We could say he never encounters people. Lifton points this out about the historical figure and mentions that the only people Mengele thought of as people were other doctors; this idea was so fixed in his mind that he would take the Jewish doctors off the ramp in Auschwitz and employ them in his laboratory. The only "people" for Mengele were doctors, doubles who allowed him to see himself as a person. Beholding his "medical" sketches in the film makes us nervous. The nervousness stems from the revelation of his medicine as uncanny, as having nothing to do with science or a shared discourse at all, but as showing evidence of a personal enjoyment—precisely the kind that science is supposed to eschew.

After receiving several injection "treatments" from the doctor, who has masked himself as a veterinarian, Lilith touches her lower abdomen to discover a rash. When she questions Mengele about the rash, he says it is a "good sign" and doubles the medicinal dose. Ignoring the real signs of disturbance—not her size but her reddened abdomen—Mengele pushes forward more excitedly with his project. The real signs of failure only spur him on, rather than providing any kind of limit. In a perverse logic, his failure only further ensures that the ideal is pursued more voraciously. The ideal is thus not subject to "reality testing"; its frustration only ensures it is held onto more tenaciously. In the romantic tradition of the mad scientist, Mengele never releases his aims for a second. Moreover, the doctor's series of injections into Lilith's pelvis and into her mother's pregnant belly are ways of making holes in them that are not sexual, holes that avoid their own feminine holes. This hole is the way he can sustain the mirror and imaginarily master the genesis of life itself without sexuality, since sexuality—a use of his own hole—would only confront him with his position as man, as mortal, and as lacking.

Mengele is also drawn to Patagonia, where, while in disguise, he stumbles upon Lilith and her family. When they meet at a filling station, the doctor asks if he can follow the family through the desert. The road on which they drive is a desert road with no markers where it is difficult to determine direction. When Mengele asks if he can follow the family, the father replies, "Foreigners are always afraid of this route."[21] This suggests that the father, who is familiar with the road already, knows Mengele is a stranger and not who he appears to be. Even though the father hesitates, he assents to the convoy, and a kind of uncanny chaperoning begins.

Enzo has been shown to be inadequate in his ability to support the family, and the trip to the mother's childhood home is a solution. As developed in *The Unconcept*, the uncanny is associated with the "notion of *Heim*, [and thus] with the secret (*Geheimnis*)."[22] The maternal home and the maternal line include Eva's deceased mother. We could suppose that the "motherland" is precisely the secret that uncannily reveals itself beneath the dream of the *Vaterland* as Freud's "return of the repressed." Significantly, this maternal home is a hotel, underlining the fact that there is no home or real belonging, even to the mother, except in death. The maternal hotel, both home and not home, is the quintessential uncanny *topos*. Mengele follows the family on the desert road to find out their secrets, and in following them, he becomes part of their secret.[23] He discovers where they are going and eventually insinuates himself as their first boarder. The stranger appears suspicious, but he offers them money—something he will do continually, a temptation they cannot refuse. Against his better judgment and conscious awareness, Enzo is able to be bought.

The uninvited guest, the doctor, makes the hotel and neighboring environs into an uncanny space for secret experiments, as well as for the secrets he keeps with the mother and with the daughter, the least of the secrets that surround his person. Even more eerie, in a further uncanny irony, the hotel resides next to a hospital for the disabled that serves as home to *both* the handicapped (the very people the Nazi doctors euthanized) *and* the escaped Nazi doctors. Still, the strange doctor is the first one to get a room, and his presence in the not-yet-open-for-business hotel threatens the family's own sense of belonging, especially as he experiments on the mother and daughter in secret. To whom do the women owe their allegiance? The family's return to the maternal homeland and family hotel provides no hoped-for belonging, but only more anxious encounters.

Historically, many Nazi refugees fled from Allied and Soviet punishment to Patagonia after the war, and some were taken in by the United States.[24] The hotel and hospital in the story are set in Bariloche, Argentina, where German immigrants lived in nostalgically constructed nineteenth-century wooden Alpine houses. Adolf Eichmann, Josef Mengele, and Erich Priebke were just some of the important high-ranking Nazi refugees who were known to have resided there.

The etymology of the word "Patagonia" means "big feet." During his circumnavigation of the globe, Magellan witnessed the inordinately tall people in that region and called them "*patagoni*" (Italian). People thought that a mythic race of giants existed in a far-off place, and this, for Jews and Christians, would recall the unexplained giants, the *Nephilim*, in the Bible (Gen. 6:4, Num. 13:33, Eze. 32:27). Patagonia, the land of giants, is ironically the very place where we meet a twelve-year-old girl who is too short! The Nazi ideology of Aryan perfection is linked to the Argentinean myth of giants, which in turn is linked to the biblical reference. Patagonia is yet an*other* potential paradise of which the Nazis could dream, a place once inhabited by giants; perhaps the *Sonnenmenschen* would be found there—and if not, they could surely engineer them. The Andes look enough like the Alps, after all.

The race of giants is always a child's wish since giants are modeled on our lost powerful parents and denote both an anxiety and marvel at their power, one we would like for our childhood selves as we look upon them with envy and awe.

The German language plays an uncanny role as that which is both "home and stranger"[25] at the same time, allowing the doctor to speak with the mother in secret, leaving the father out. As a girl, Eva had learned German in Bariloche at her mother's hotel. When the family first arrives there, Eva pulls out photos of herself at age ten and shows them to her daughter Lilith. These pictures are evidence of Eva's having grown up as *both* Argentine and German.[26] Bariloche is where she learned to speak the language and where all the students were saluting "*Heil Hitler*" during the early 1940s. When Mengele realizes the wife speaks his language, he asks her quietly whether her husband understands them. Enzo overhears, and in an ironic reply, intones that he does not understand at all. Eva and Mengele communicate their secret fertility assistance plans beyond the reach of the father's purview. As in Hoffmann's "The Sandman," again we note the two "fathers": Enzo, the biological father of the children, is also the father-maker of the doll. The "father" of "perfected children" and of mass-produced dolls, however, is the German doctor.[27]

Mengele convinces Eva that he should treat Lilith with bovine hormone and shows her charts that depict her daughter as abnormal. He convinces Eva that Lilith should receive hormones even though Enzo has expressly forbidden it. His wife meets with the doctor in secret and proceeds to ignore Enzo's rule. A devoted mother, Eva will do anything for her daughter. Even when Enzo reminds his wife that Mengele is not their family doctor, she is nevertheless persuaded by Mengele, who promises he can abolish Lilith's "deformity" and fortify her unborn twins. The partner of the psychotic doctor with "the answer" is the mother's wish for healthy, and more importantly, "normal" children.

While Eva and Enzo have a happy marriage, in a move that undermines her trust with her husband, Eva subscribes to Mengele's promise of paradise and narcissistic tyranny where the psychotic gives back the phallus to the mother. Mengele promises to "abolish the cosmic polarity of the male and female principles." This promise is related to the metamorphosis of the mother and daughter into "complete life forms," restoring them literally, including Lilith's size, in a disregard of neurotic lack.

The doctor promises Lilith that she will grow to be one of the *Sonnenmenschen*; the dwarf shall become a giant. Fascinated by the drawings she finds in a Nazi book hidden in the library and by her promised place, Lilith believes in Mengele's treatment. She wants to be the fantasy object for the "*Ur Vater*" and we see how this is imbricated in separating from and relating to her phallic place for her mother. Lilith asks the librarian about the meaning of *Sonnenmenschen* when she can't find the word in the dictionary—already an important moment since the word is not part of a shared vocabulary. This question introduces a key character in the film, the librarian and archivist who gives Lilith information about Nazi "supermen." Nora Eldoc is a figure taken from history. In the film, she is on the side of meaning and the symbolic for the girl and allows her to begin to question the message she has received from this seemingly all-powerful Other.

Nora Eldoc is first introduced to the family in Bariloche at an inaugural school party. The adult double of Lilith, she functions as an antidote to the doll. She is also, importantly, a double agent who works for the Mossad[28] and, as such, places a limit to the overriding theme of the uncanny, since despite being "double," her affiliation is nevertheless clear. She provides bits of information to Lilith about Mengele and helps her realize the pernicious and threatening nature of his experiments. Nora secretly takes photographs of Mengele, eventually reporting his presence to the Israeli authorities. From the beginning, Mengele suspects Nora of not being "one of us" and asks his comrade whether she is trustworthy. He is able to recognize his adversary *as a woman* who thinks and who knows—a woman who sees and is not blinded by any phallic desire to belong. A woman who is no longer a child threatens him. We could say that only with the wishes of a child does the doctor have a place with women at all. The historic Mengele was famous for his ability to see "through" others. Even an assistant who worked for him and other doctors at Auschwitz, and who claimed that it was easy to manipulate the doctors and get them to do what she wanted, said of the particularity of Mengele, "I don't think for a moment that I could manipulate him, ever ever."[29] People intuited that it was not possible to fool him, and it was simply more expedient to tell him the truth as often as possible.

Nora Eldoc's photos function to create a record of Mengele, who was thought by many to be lost or dead. After she is sent a letter that says (in code) that Eichmann is about to be arrested, she carries on photographing Mengele with renewed verve. We see Eldoc's "project" as the antipode to the doctor's; they both become more impassioned after they see the real effects of their work: he by the rash on Lilith's abdomen, she by the knowledge that Eichmann has been captured and that spying can result in capturing a criminal. Eldoc compiles a record to expose Mengele's identity and whereabouts. This will cost her her life.[30] Mengele attempts to displace such identification as deceitful, by ensuring that it is Nora who remains the dangerous threat.

In the film, Mengele literally and physically twists Nora's arm and threatens her life while the frightened Lilith looks on, unseen by either of them. The girl's observation of this scene is a turning point in the story where she becomes skeptical and even fearful of the doctor since she identifies with Nora and trusts her. After witnessing this scene, Lilith follows Mengele up to his office where he is packing his bags. The doctor senses their "relationship" is about to come to an end and asks Lilith if she would "do anything" for him. For the first time, she answers no. In response, he does not ask why or what's wrong, but decrees: "You will not forget me."

It will in fact be hard for the family to "forget" the experiments done on the twins, Eva, or Lilith as they have a permanent effect on their bodies. Nora Eldoc opens Mengele's journal to the uncanny sketches of deformity and of the family, including drawings of the twins, Enzo, Eva, and Lilith. The journal reveals how the doctor thrives on manipulating the Real to rid the world of its supposed deformity. Nora shows Enzo the journal with drawings of his own head, indicating its size and diameter. She shows him the doctor's drawings of his wife depicted naked and pregnant. The journal reveals that Mengele has been experimenting on the twins, with one baby as a control for the other. Nora Eldoc's evidence finally convinces Enzo of Mengele's identity, and he realizes in quiet horror what has transpired between Mengele and the women in his family. In this way, Nora shows how Mengele is an imposter in Patagonia. In terms of the narrative of the film, while Mengele promises an ideal-ego, Nora's symbolic work allows her to become an ego-ideal for Lilith, which ultimately constructs a document (photos, film) that shows Mengele's true character.

When Mengele proposes the mass production of dolls to Enzo, he offers Enzo a particular role: no longer the maker of each doll individually, he will have the role in the proposed new company of winding up every mass-produced doll's heart and placing it inside the doll's torso himself. A perverse and literally Faustian offer, in exchange for financial gain, Enzo will have to bear the fact that such mass-produced dolls will nonetheless have hearts—and Enzo will become, since he was the one who put them there, an artist reduced to a "heart giver" on an assembly line. Enzo will be made to realize what he has done when he goes to the factory and sees the monstrous rows of heads, legs, and torsos all detached. Mengele has turned his beloved artistic creation into a mass-produced doll, now a fragmented body—and he has done the same with his treatments of Eva and Lilith. Ultimately, when Enzo realizes his mistake, he tells Lilith she doesn't need the treatments; she doesn't need to be perfect; there is always someone taller, blonder, or more "perfect." The father shows his daughter how the dream of bodily perfection is a fallacy by relishing each idiosyncrasy of each doll, and he encourages her to enjoy her own differences and to consider these imperfections as what makes her unique, like Wakolda.

The doctor says that "hereditary diseases skip a generation," but "you must be careful it could happen again." The fear of genetic inheritance has effectively replaced mothering as symbolic with mothering as biological. One is no longer held to any symbolic authority to produce ethical subjects; one's role is completely reduced to an imaginary vigilance. Who needs parents at all?

In the end, the film shows how Mengele's experiments on the woman's body, with her complicity, cause real damage. Enzo realizes there is nothing he can do to get Mengele out of his house when, due to the storm, they must ask Mengele to deliver the twins. He further realizes how Mengele has actually gotten inside the bodies of his wife and daughter—a realization of the uncanny breaching of the "*heim*" and of his own powerlessness.

Mengele would like to continue working on Eva's twins, but he realizes he must decamp after a nurse informs him that Eichmann has been captured and he is in danger. When the nurse presses him to leave, he replies: "Not yet, my work here is not done!" He believes so much in his "calling" that he is ready to sacrifice himself for it. At this point, the babies are in plastic bags making an oxygen bubble. Looking apprehensively at her suffering newborns, Eva says that the babies are "best off with him [Mengele]," adding, "I don't care who he is!" Enzo replies importantly, "*I do*." The scene shows the place the newborns have for their mother, one wherein she would sacrifice her symbolic and ethical position and do anything to keep them alive. This is clearly not Enzo's position. It cannot be.

Lilith's "no" to the doctor, and Enzo's caution not to "do anything for the children" marks the end of the film—a limit is made. Lifton opines that "the Auschwitz self was the means by which the Nazi doctor could bring to his killing the mana of a shaman, a priest, a magician."[31] The "Patagonia self" was the means by which the Nazi doctor made it even more clear that the self is already Other—and that shamans, priests, and magicians can only work their magic in fairy tales,[32] travel logs, or concentration camps. In Patagonia, the "Nazi biological revolutionary" that Mengele "exemplifies" is revealed as less magical, less shamanistic, and more simply what he was—criminally insane.[33] If, as one prisoner doctor testified about the infamous doctor, "He had no problems—not with his conscience, not with anybody, not with anything" in exile and in disguise, others had problems with him.[34] Ultimately, the film shows us that there is no self and there is no belonging, despite the power of the Nazi imaginary. In the end, the father finally acts on what he sees—and the daughter does the same to grow up, become a woman, and write the novel. To find one's proper place, then, concerns the loss of paradise and the invention of a limit via aesthetic engagement. Instead of "belonging" in some maternal uncanny paradise, the film shows Mengele's promise of perfection as ersatz; only death belongs there.

NOTES

1. This chapter began as a film review in a shorter version as "Belonging is Uncanny: *Wakolda*, or *The German Doctor*," by Jessica Datema and Manya Steinkoler in *The Candidate: Perspectives from an Evolving Psychoanalytic Community* 6 (2015).

2. Lucía Puenzo, *Wakolda*, trans. David William Foster (London: Hesperus Press, 2014); Lucía Puenzo, dir., *The German Doctor*, 2014.

3. Robert Jay Lifton, *The Nazi Doctors: Medical Killing and the Psychology of Genocide* (New York: Basic Books, 2017), 353.
4. Lifton, *Nazi Doctors*, 343, 356.
5. Lifton, *Nazi Doctors*, 338.
6. Puenzo, *Wakolda*, 69.
7. Puenzo, *Wakolda*, 56.
8. Jane Martinson, "American Girl Is Beating Barbie—and I'm Celebrating," *The Guardian*, July 22, 2013, https://www.theguardian.com/lifeandstyle/the-womens-blog-with-jane-martinson/2013/jul/22/american-girl-beating-barbie-celebrating.
9. Lifton, *Nazi Doctors*, 359.
10. Puenzo, *Wakolda*, 48.
11. E. T. A. Hoffmann, Leonard J. Kent, and Elizabeth C. Knight, *Tales of E. T. A. Hoffmann* (Chicago: University of Chicago Press, 1974), 103.
12. Lifton, *Nazi Doctors*, 372.
13. Lifton, *Nazi Doctors*, 374.
14. Lifton, *Nazi Doctors*, 343.
15. Lifton, *Nazi Doctors*, 353.
16. Lifton, *Nazi Doctors*, 359.
17. Lifton, *Nazi Doctors*, 346.
18. Lucette Lagnado and Sheila Cohn Dekel, *Children of the Flames: Dr. Josef Mengele and the Untold Story of the Twins of Auschwitz* (New York: Penguin Books, 1992).
19. Lifton, *Nazi Doctors*, 360.
20. Jacques Lacan, "Petit Discours Aux Psychiatres," November 10, 1967, http //ali-aix-salon.com/J.Lacan%20Conf.%20sur%20la%20Psychanalyse%20et%20formation%20psychiatre%201967.pdf.
21. Puenzo, *Wakolda*, 24.
22. Anneleen Masschelein, *Unconcept: The Freudian Uncanny in Late-Twenieth-Century Theory* (Albany: SUNY, 2012), 57.
23. Slavoj Žižek, *Welcome to the Desert of the Real: Five Essays on September 11 and Related Dates* (London : Verso, 2002), 15.
24. Eric Lichtblau, "In Cold War, U.S. Spy Agencies Used 1,000 Nazis," *The New York Times*, October 26, 2014.
25. Masschelein, *Unconcept*.
26. "Just Following Orders: Erich Priebke," *The Economist*, October 26, 2013.
27. Hoffmann et al., *Tales*, 93.
28. "Interview with Mossad Agent: 'We Could Have Killed Mengele,'" *Spiegel Online*, September 8, 2008, http://www.spiegel.de/international/world/interview-with-mossad-agent-we-could-have-killed-mengele-a-576973.html.
29. Lifton, *Nazi Doctors*, 344.
30. "Israeli Woman Killed by Nazis in Argentina; Sought Nazi War Criminal," *Jewish Telegraphic Agency*, March 22, 1961, http://www.jta.org/1961/03/22/archive/israeli-woman-killed-by-nazis-in-argentina-sought-nazi-war-criminal.
31. Lifton, *Nazi Doctors*, 427.
32. Bruno Bettelheim, *The Uses of Enchantment: The Meaning and Importance of Fairy Tales* (New York: Random House Inc, 2010).
33. Lifton, *Nazi Doctors*, 377.
34. Lifton, *Nazi Doctors*, 344.

Chapter Three

Phoenix

The After-Death

If the Holocaust has alerted us to the insufficiency of representation and the concomitant impossibility of language to bear the Real,[1] Christian Petzold's film *Phoenix* (2015) allows us to reexamine these assumptions and think of these limitations in a new way. The film alerts us to the way immanent subjectivity and traumatic agency are birthed from an impossible history. It shows the transformative power of art, both as a film and in terms of its themes. By way of form and content, the film, true to its name, births new possibilities arising from the faceless ashes of death. It reinvents the Holocaust and questions of representation beyond the much-bemoaned problems of narrative, or the famous Lanzmannian "sacred impossibility of representation," to pose a complex ethics of survival (*Shoah*).[2] The invention the film proposes is perverse but results in a new post-mortem agency. As a Holocaust narrative, *Phoenix* is ultimately concerned with survival as linked to disinheritance and dispossession that results from the foreclosure of history.

The film shows the reduction of the subject to the Real, bereft of any symbolic or imaginary veil, much like the raped women in *A Woman in Berlin.* All the representations and possibilities the world provides, and most importantly love—love that is the very glue that allows a world to hold together—have been stolen, the flesh numbed and cauterized from these innumerable and unnamable losses. The protagonist, Nelly, played by Nina Hoss, returns from the camps, coming back to life as herself in a post-mortem perverse staging to ascertain if there is any love left after being betrayed and sent to Auschwitz by her wastrel "accompanist" of a husband, his cruel abandonment ironically revealing the collaborationist in the word "accompanist." When she returns, Nelly is a woman worn down to the bone, to the barest minimal self, by an impossible history.

Nelly's exile is the way the filmmaker asks us to look at ourselves and our contemporary "non-social link," as it unmasks the symbolic, revealing it as a fiction. While Lacan tells us the symbolic is a fiction, part of any analytic cure underlines that it is a fiction we need, and one made possible by love. Nelly uses a masochistic staging to survive the horror that the societal fiction has become, hoping that love will make that fiction bearable once again, only to discover its absolute collapse. The genius of the film is that the problematics of representation—especially as they concern the Holocaust—are worked through in the narrative and the masochistic mise-en-scène itself. *Phoenix* answers the question "How is it possible to put a face on death?" The answer is by way of artistic reconstruction.

The film is the medium by which the mythic phoenix transformation can take place, because after all, a film is a "moving reel." In this sense, the film narrates its own birth and destruction by way of a literal bright light that bookends the story. This blinding light reveals a *jouissance* residing outside the frame: death as real and death as the ultimate "knowledge" beyond all sight, beyond all insight, and beyond all film. Fire destroys the phoenix and, at the same time, fire is the cause of its birth. Bachelard asserts that fire is an object whose "initial charm . . . is so strong that it still has the power to warp the minds of the clearest thinkers."[3] Already for Bachelard, fire connotes the unthinkable. His famous text highlights the relation of fire as an object of prohibition, desire, knowledge, empowerment, and therefore transformation.

For Lacan, fire concerns the Real. In his *Seminar VII: Ethics*, Lacan refers to the burning bush as Moses's Thing.[4] Later, in *Seminar XI*, in his reading of the dream, "Father can't you see I'm burning," he writes that "this sentence is itself a fire-brand—of itself it brings fire where it falls—and one cannot see what is burning, for the flames blind us to the fact that the fire bears on the *Unterlegt*, on the *Untertragen*, on the real."[5] The fire is the *Real* of the dream, that reality to which the father does not want to awake, a reality of pure loss. This is the bad dream into which Nelly steps when she returns to Berlin. The situation in Germany is one of pure loss, being beyond the ability to restore law. If the Holocaust was named for a consuming fire that burns the whole, *Phoenix* makes a non-final solution out of the final solution, allowing a future to rise up from these ashes.

The rebirth potential in *Phoenix* is certainly not obvious, and the modern use of imaginary Band-Aids as ego defenses in our contemporary world parallels what happens initially in the film. Even though it is set in the post-Holocaust era, the film foregrounds the normative state of culture in twenty-first century globalization, where the individual is reduced to symbolic chaff or what W. H. Auden had already, almost a century ago, called an "Unknown Citizen."[6] *Phoenix* asks what cultural inheritance is left for Germany and for the Jewish people after the Holocaust. The film shows that statehood is in no way a solution to the problem the film poses; nationalism only repeats the crisis, allowing an imaginary group identity to congeal and persist, thus prescribing, murdering, or foreclosing all "Otherness." The film also asks us what cultural future we have been destined to and are living in right now as a result of these events.

After the war, Germany is shrouded in an imaginary narrative regarding its immediate past, where culpability is ineffectively but forcibly foreclosed. The film makes clear that as a result of the catastrophe, Germans are just as disinherited as Jewish survivors, asking us to think of the Germans as deposed as well, even if their sense of belonging and nationhood as dissolved is initially unbeknownst to them. Nelly, like her people, is betrayed by her beloved husband and thus can no longer return to her prior self; however, after the war, Germans were not only hated, but when the foreclosure was finally revealed both to them and to the world, they became eternally culpable, permanently fixed, and like Nelly's husband Johnny, turned to stone beholding their own monster. What does the future hold after one turns to stone?

Phoenix reflects what is in play in our contemporary moment: a deadness and loss of the sense of being a part of a shared social meaning. We "live" as numbered and alienated citizens with a sense that we are only performing ourselves. Nelly performs for the one who has betrayed her and has sent her to the gas chamber. Yet this masochistic staging indicts the entire world that perpetrated genocide and produced refugees. She exposes Germany's mistake in attempting to "have done" with the Jew, the refugee—and, we could add, to have done with the woman. The name Nelly is a diminutive of Helen; it means torch or shining light. Her name connects her to national narrative and epic war, as well as to the bird whose name the film takes as its title. Like Helen of Troy, who is also Helen of Sparta and Helen of Egypt, woman defies being "placed"; like the phoenix, she is timeless and other to herself. Just like the ancient beauty she is named after, Nellie defies country, topos, and notions of presence.

In this sense, Nelly stands for that Thing that is *not* any woman in particular but the Other qua abject citizen for global society, *Homo Sacer*, the scapegoat, or simply "the feminine" as that which cannot be represented. Nelly's return, like "Antigone's act, is meant to 'rescue' the Symbolic from the 'criminal' universalization of the law; she nevertheless ends up embodying one of the most tangible fulfillments of the Sado-Kantian imperative."[7] What Chiesa calls the "Sado-Kantian imperative" is Nelly's masochistic "act," one that we have mentioned displays a complex ethics, much like Lacan's Antigone in *Seminar VII*, or like what Agamben calls the *Homo Sacer*. Nelly is a real ethical figure that is erased in history but returns to indict it. If, for Agamben, the ethics of testimony involves the Muselmann—

that is, the walking dead who cannot testify—then Nelly is the uncanny Muselmann who remains to testify.[8]

Out of this monolithic eternity of the reifying of the subject as chaff, as garbage, as flesh for manufacturing use, the *Phoenix* is born. The phoenix makes a series possible in infinity; in this sense, it is Sinthomatic because it involves aesthetic creation from a void. The time presented in the film is infinite time: Nelly is a living corpse and German culpability is eternal. The film shows her returned with her face blown off, uncannily having survived the camps, in the way anyone "survived them"—that is, without a face. Much of the film's action takes place in a Berlin nightclub named Phoenix, set in the American occupied territory. The nightclub carries on the horror and squalor of postwar Germany with cabaret singers and ex-Nazis waiting tables. It is a place that purports to be in neutral territory but seems to be an extension of decadent prewar Berlin as though nothing happened. The film's setting includes noir elements, such as the nightclub's name Phoenix, which is illuminated as a neon sign and casts a lurid red glow on the ruined city streets. The permanence of German denial is present in the Weimar-ish setting, as is the idea that while everything has changed, nothing has changed at all.

Phoenix plays with stereotypical noir forms of glossiness and monstrosity, including Nelly's reconstructed face, as evidence of Holocaust crime. When the film begins, Nelly is without a face, literally a ghost. Her head is covered in white bandages like a mummy after days of recuperating from surgery. Significantly, Nelly's face is not visible until well into the film, and we are left wondering, like her: Who is she? She walks around the hospital like a phantom, wearing a shroud, mute, unable to speak or sing, a shade. When the bandages finally come off, Nelly is a visage of real postwar refuse come back to haunt Berlin after being expelled. The dead live.

The masochistic staging begins when she goes back to find Johnny after healing from surgery and receiving an artificial visage. The plastic surgeon advises Nelly to take a new face in order to remain unidentifiable, but she refuses and requests a mask that is an exact replica of her former self so as to be able to perform herself even more perfectly. Her request—to become what she was—shows that her identity is lost. Nelly already wants to return to Johnny even though she may have intuited that the imaginary is a construct—and not a secure one—following trauma.

Restored, Nelly goes to the nightclub to figure out what Johnny is up to, but also to figure out who she is, who she was, and who she has become after being interned in the camps. When she arrives at Phoenix, Cole Porter's "Night and Day" is being sung while Nelly sees Johnny washing dishes. She calls out his name, but he looks up at the sound of her voice without recognition. It's unclear whether he recognizes her or not because the name he has taken after the war is "Johannes"; he has become someone else because of what he did. When Johnny turns his back on her to resume cleaning, Nelly runs out, returning to her apartment where she stares sadly into a full-length mirror; losing Johnny, she has lost herself. Without his love, she has no idea who she is.

Nelly's postsurgical visage oscillates uncannily between appearing—like Germany after 1945—as a reconstruction and a re-creation. By simply appearing, she destroys Germany's exonerating face-saving fantasy. We are reminded of the mirror stage as supporting fantasy—in this case, as upholding the symbolic edifice as constructed by fantasy itself. Nelly's love for Johnny allows her to become a "likeness" of herself. Nelly's very countenance mocks the notion that everyone can "put on his or her best face" as a kind of macabre absurd. The initial idea of a solution is one where she takes the same face, seeking restoration of her real body, singing voice, and love relationship before the camps—as if getting her prewar self back would reinstall a wished-for past. Even after the imaginary has already been stripped away, Nelly hopes it can be found again or revived by love with the partner she longed for during her internment. The irony, of course, is that the symbolic fiction has been totally destroyed. As a literal mask of her former self, a kind of heroic Perseus, Nelly indicts Germany's monstrosity. This recalls Anonyma's husband's return in *A Woman in Berlin*, which can only result in his rejection and flight.

Discovering that the symbolic is a lie, Nelly is reduced to a semblance of her lost self and finds that her identity, her husband, and her country were never what she thought they were in the first place. This is the beginning of the transformation of the phoenix. After finding Johnny, she imitates his "lost wife" and takes the name Esther. Esther, as anyone knows from the story of the Purim holiday, was the Jewish wife who replaced Vashti, the queen of the Persian king Ahasueros.[9] Esther saves the Jews by intervening and beseeching the king, her husband, on their behalf. Significantly, Nelly's choice of "Esther" as her stage name is strangely true, as she stands for the Holocaust victims that rise out of the ashes. As Nelly's "false name," Esther is truer than Nelly; it is the imitation that is the supposed truth of herself. Already, by way of her chosen stage name, her position as post-traumatic agent trumps her imaginary aims. We note the similarity of Marta Hillers's pen name Anonyma, a similar invention to recount the atrocities of rape in postwar Berlin.[10]

Even if Johnny suspects that Esther is Nelly, or that the woman acting as his lost wife is actually his wife, he never lets on. His "knowing ignorance" is interesting to reflect upon. If he knows, he enjoys the sadism; if he doesn't know, he enjoys getting away with it. No matter what his position, he thinks he is putting one over on the authorities and identifies, like Esther, with the one who "puts one over" on someone else. In this sense, he has something in common with his wife; both are playing perversely to deal with a collapsed symbolic world.

In one particularly masochistic scene, Johnny asks Esther to imitate the handwriting of his ex-wife Nelly by copying a shopping list. After he leaves her with this task, Esther looks around his house, peeking into his drawers, using a knife to pick a lock. The locked space opens to a piano and a trunk with Nelly's old clothes. She is looking for herself and she signs herself, and in imitating her old signature, she loses herself in the process. After Johnny inspects her obviously impeccable work, he has the bright idea that they could stage the retrieval of his wife to get hold of her inheritance, and he commands her to pen "I am alive and well in Zurich, will return soon, Nelly." Of course, Esther's writing is identical to Nelly's because it is an imitation that is authentic. In this sense, Esther's handwriting is more satisfying to Johnny than his own wife's real signature could ever possibly be, because via Esther he gets to think that his "putting one over" is viable, and he not only gets a perverse satisfaction out of outsmarting the other, but he gets to steal the sought-after inheritance. By the end, when Nelly appears as herself, she is radiant and unscarred by the camps—as if life now, in the past, and in the future, was, is, and will be just hunky-dory.

Johnny wants to claim Nelly's financial inheritance; in this way as well, she is reduced to a number, a fiduciary one. She is not only phoenix, but "fee-nix," showing a debt that is infinite and cannot be remunerated. Nelly returns to Germany without any family but with a massive inheritance, a horrific excess made possible by her family's mass murder. The compounded betrayal of her to the Nazis and absconding with her inheritance is a way of continuing to kill her as an instance of *hainamoration* (love-hate). Correlatively, Johnny's repugnant coveting of Nelly's inheritance does not belie his love, despite what a naiver audience might think. His love is "composed of the noun *haine* (hate) and the adjective *énamoré*" at one and the same time.[11] Ironically, this is how he is most clearly her lover and deadly accompanist—the one who never leaves the side of the one they have to kill. Just as the "chosen people" and the "premiere Aryan race" are enmeshed in such a *hainamoration*, so Johnny and Nelly are in a love-death match. Nelly was not naive to have imagined Johnny's love; Johnny loved her in the particular and passionate way that one loves when one kills.

Love on the side of death is contrasted with phoenix as love on the side of life. This reading of the phoenix is present in the Jewish midrash tradition, where we note a monotheistic interpretation of the pagan myth. The medieval rabbis link the phoenix not to knowledge but to love. For the rabbis, influenced by the Hellenistic tradition and by the early Christianity that they abjure, the phoenix lives because it did not eat from the tree of knowledge. Thus, it avoids death and symbolic law. We could argue that in the film, although Nelly left Johnny's love, she never left love, thus she lives again, like the mythic bird.

It is interesting to consider that Lilith and phoenix are two apocryphal "characters" that are both biblical and post-biblical; they are midrashic constructions aimed at thinking about an outside of the fall. In *Etourdit*, Lacan's difficult 1973 reflection on the anti-Aristotelian logic of psychoanalysis, he underscores that death is not simply a universal.[12] In a logic particular to Lacanian psychoanalysis, there is a modal preface to all "universal" statements that make them impossible. Lacan is aiming at the "immortality" of art through possibility—that is, the after death.

Their masochistic staging continues the next day when Johnny puts out Nelly's clothes for Esther. Esther wears Nelly's shoes and, like Cinderella's glass slipper, they fit perfectly. Nevertheless, she walks slowly and tentatively until Johnny directs her to proceed more sturdily. Frustrated, he declares: "Do the shoes pinch? Why are you walking strangely—walk normal!" This awkward moment "in her own shoes" shows both her hesitancy to continue the charade, as well as the fact that her own shoes no longer "fit" even if they do "fit perfectly." Or we could say, "If the shoe fits, *don't* wear it!" Life is not a fairy tale. Not only does Esther don Nelly's shoes, she will put on her dress and eventually dye her hair and apply makeup to look exactly like his wife. This after Johnny declares that Esther looks "awful" and should "imitate a picture" that looks like Nelly. Johnny's perverse entreaty is not attainable, but Esther does her best to "imitate."

This scene alludes to film history, with Johnny in this perverse position imitating "Johnny" in Hitchcock's *Vertigo*.[13] While Hitchcock's film focuses on the fall, *Phoenix* focuses on the rising. After finally transforming into Nelly, the staging is temporarily suspended when Esther wonders what she should say should anyone inquire about what happened to Nelly in the camps. "No one wants to know about that; no one will ever want to hear about that," her erstwhile husband retorts. The covering up of Nelly's time in the camp is part of the perverse staging to conceal a greater crime. The staging not only functions to continue their masquerade of love, but it portends a perverse aspect of our own society and postmodern culture where we are all "putting one over" on each *other* because of an increasing symbolic breakdown and ensuing anxiety.

Nelly exposes not only the tragedy of Nazi atrocities and her lost love, but the situation of being an unknown citizen. Her face covers a greater criminal horror "beyond tragedy," where she, like Antigone, is a sublime figure whose "place occupies an intermediary between two fields that are symbolically differentiated. It is from this place that her splendor derives."[14] Those are the two places of the phoenix. Nelly occupies the beyond of representation in tragedy whose reconstructed face is an uncanny sublime apparition of "something entirely different."[15] Tragedy is that genre wherein one learns what one knows but does not want to know; tragedy is public and involves hubris—in this case, Johnny's and the Germans'. In tragedy, the tragic hero has to make an impossible choice, as Nelly does. However, the film is a perverse staging *beyond* tragedy: first, because genocidal death happened before the film began, and if tragedy, as Lacan tells us, takes place "between two deaths," this film takes place *after* the second one. Finally, the film is unlike tragedy because *Phoenix* is a symbol of the *beyond* of tragedy—that is, the transformative power of life, of an after-death and a not-yet-known. The future is that which will be created. Being over, it has just begun.

In Jacques-Alain Miller's reading of Borges's short story "The Sect of the Phoenix," he shows that for Lacan, the phoenix is the phallus, which he calls "the hatchet of history."[16] He compares the sect of the phoenix to the secrets revealed in analysis—secrets that, like sex, make no chronological or signifying sense. In this manner, the analytic space is the space of the phoenix insofar as it allows for subjective rebirth. The analytic session is a place of witnessing to erased history, where unspoken desire and *jouissance* condescend to speech. The time of the session, like the time of *Revisioning War Trauma* films, is one where the infinity of myth becomes subject to the finitude of punctuation in relation to symbolization.

Phoenix presents time as the "hatchet of history," in a way that can be juxtaposed with Norman Bates's obsession with birds. We recall that Hitchcock's *Psycho* takes place in Phoenix, Arizona. Norman lives in a "Motherland," without history, in an off-the-lost-highway of perpetual *jouissance*. Unlike Nelly, Norman can never be reborn, only transformed into his mother; here the *jouissance* is eternal. Even before Petzold, Hitchcock shows that America is not the answer to postwar malaise.

Nelly's return, like Eurydice, is an uncanny homecoming that no one anticipates or knows how to handle. *Phoenix* stages history as foreclosed, and thus her return is traumatic. She is "the survivor [who] becomes the repetition of the reality that consciousness cannot grasp. In the traumatic encounter with death, life itself attempts to serve as the witness that consciousness cannot provide."[17] The film uses Nelly's return as an artistic interruption or one way to bear witness to the face of the Other—in the Levianasian sense. This Other forces a confrontation with the real of the camps, namely an Other without a face, the Other that can have no face.

In the film's final scene, the masquerade is unveiled at the moment Nelly sings Kurt Weill's "Speak Low." In this scene, the truth about Nelly—that she has both died and survived the camps—becomes real; she *is* the phoenix. Her singing voice gives her away and is how recognition occurs after the disaster. Phoenix is found in her voice that is reborn after being consumed by the flames; as fire uses air, so does the real use the voice. Nelly's singing also indicts the entire listening and viewing audience as implicated in the Nazi cover-up, thereby bequeathing to them the eternity Nelly suffered alone. The music in the film is not the real voice of Nelly; it is the voice of the voiceless who died or nearly died in the camps, or were forced to leave Germany, like Kurt Weill himself. This voice cannot be reconstructed or foreclosed; the survivor's material body remains. Giving voice to the voiceless, Nelly walks into a blinding white light; she *is* the phoenix.

At this precise moment, Johnny, transfixed and destroyed, stops accompanying Nelly, who is still singing as our gaze falls upon the tattoo of her camp number. The number is burned onto her arm, attesting to Germany's crimes and Johnny's betrayal. Earlier in the film, he tried to get rid of the evidence, asking Nelly to cut the tattoo out of her skin in a cruel, repeated vivisection of her camp experience. Her refusal is the sign of her rebirth. The decision to keep her tattoo comes after Nelly becomes cognizant of the divorce papers, which her friend Lena, who commits suicide, gave to her posthumously. These documents ensure that she has no choice but to recognize her husband's betrayal. At this moment, she realizes the futility of her act. The masochistic staging of her former self can in no way bring back the love she had hoped to recapture, the hope that kept her alive during the war. After this, when Johnny and Nelly sing the lyrics of "Speak Low," she has already decided to expose the very tattoo that Johnny wanted to excise, the scar of history itself. This exposure speaks the unspeakable; it testifies to the "low" voices of the voiceless that postwar Germany cannot simply deny.

An*other* way of looking at *Phoenix* is via Walter Benjamin's discussion of Paul Klee's painting *Angelus Novus* in his essay "Theses on the Philosophy of History." Benjamin's angel, like Nelly, is a witness to catastrophe upon catastrophe and the traumatic violence of history perversely considered to be "progress." In Benjamin's description, the angel, like Nelly, is a phoenix:

> His face is turned toward the past. Where we perceive a chain of events, he sees one single catastrophe, which keeps piling wreckage upon wreckage and hurls it in front of his feet. The angel would like to stay, awaken the dead, and make whole what has been smashed. But a storm is blowing from Paradise; it has got caught in his wings with such violence that the angel can no longer close them. The storm irresistibly propels him into the future.[18]

After the final scene singing "Speak Low," Nelly, our angel of history, is also courageously propelled into an uncertain future and an unknown country. The phoenix is reborn through light and darkness, through fire and ash, through the chiaroscuro of the film.

The ending of the film shows the mythic nature of history, beyond the impossibility and failures of the symbolic. Light and dark as revelation and occlusion is part of the motif repeatedly used throughout the film. Like Klee's angel painting, *Phoenix* shows a real history and series of disasters where the exiled citizen reduced to subjective destitution rises from the ashes to become reborn again and again. Nelly's struggle and release puts an end to romantic notions of statehood as well as ideal love. *Phoenix* shows we can only use myth if useful in the midst of symbolic breakdown as a form of storytelling that concerns the real.

In our contemporary moment, history and identity have been reduced to branding and market value. We don't wear numbers tattooed by the state; as social subjects, we *are* numbers made for markets and marketing—that is, for the fee-nix, the perverse underside that is late capital. Such contemporary dis-inheritance has no substance except the imaginary and asks the subject to conform entirely on that level, to match up with his social number. Instead of a postmodern recovery of the imaginary and reinstating the symbolic fiction, *Phoenix* asks us to be reborn beyond imaginary belonging, into a future of real hospitality we cannot yet envision, to see beyond the fiery light that has blinded us.

NOTES

1. George Steiner, *Language and Silence: Essays on Language, Literature, and the Inhuman* (New York: Atheneum, 1967), 4. "We cannot pretend that Belsen is irrelevant to the responsible life of the imagination. What man has inflicted upon man, in very recent time, has affected the writer's primary material—the sum and potential of human behavior—and it presses on the brain with a new darkness."
2. Claude Lanzmann, dir., *Shoah*, 1985.
3. Gaston Bachelard, *The Psychoanalysis of Fire*, ed. Northrop Frye, 2015, 2.
4. Jacques Lacan, "The Splendor of Antigone," in *The Ethics of Psychoanalysis: 1959–1960. The Seminar of Jacques Lacan, VII* (New York: W. W. Norton, 1978), 243–56.
5. Jacques Lacan, *The Four Fundamental Concepts of Psychoanalysis*, trans. Jacques-Alain Miller, *The Seminar of Jacques Lacan, XI* (New York: W. W. Norton, 1998), 59.
6. Wystan Hugh Auden, "The Unknown Citizen," in *Selected Poems* (New York: Vintage International, 2007), 93.
7. Lorenzo Chiesa, *Subjectivity and Otherness: A Philosophical Reading of Lacan* (Cambridge, MA: MIT Press, 2007), 182.
8. The uncanny presence of the real Muslim in Western societies today has sadly taken up such a place, as scapegoat and radical Other.
9. Esther is from the Persian, Ishtar, which is from the Semitic and Babylonian, Innana. She is the goddess of love, fertility, and war. Famously, she makes a voyage to the underworld and returns, in one of the earliest instances of such a myth. The myth, like the Demeter-Persephone myth later in Greece, connotes generation and destruction, a cyclical event, like the phoenix. The myth has been explained to suggest that "sometimes life is just not fair."
10. Anonymous, *A Woman in Berlin: Eight Weeks in the Conquered City: A Diary*, trans. Philip Boehm and Marta Hillers (New York: Picador/Henry Holt, 2006) (see chapter 1 in this book).
11. Jacques Lacan, *On Feminine Sexuality: The Limits of Love and Knowledge*, trans. Jacques Alain Miller, vol. 20, *The Seminar of Jacques Lacan, XX* (New York: W. W. Norton, 1999), 90.
12. Jacques Lacan, "L'étourdit," *Autres Écrits*, 1973, 449–95.
13. Alfred Hitchcock, dir., *Vertigo*, 1958. Doubling and substitutional identities are filmic themes and there are two of many characters in the film. In addition to Esther/Nelly there are Johannes and Johnny; both work at the nightclub, and Nelly gets them confused as she searches for him. Also, the doubling is not just in the characters; this is a film based on a film. Petzold's

film *Phoenix* is based on the French novel by Hubert Monteilhet, *Return from the Ashes* (Panther, 1965), which was made into a largely forgotten British *policier* starring Ingrid Thulin and Maximilian Schell, and directed by J. Lee Thompson (*Return from the Ashes*, 1966).

14. Jacques Lacan, *The Ethics of Psychoanalysis, 1959–1960*, vol. 7, *The Seminar of Jacques Lacan, VII* (New York: W. W. Norton, 1997), 248.

15. Lacan, *Seminar VII*, 52.

16. "Enigmatized Coitus: A Reading of Borges," in *L'orientation lacanienne*, II, 3, "Les us du laps" (November 24, 1999), delivered in the context of the Département de Psychanalyse de Paris VIII, translated from "Le coit estigmatis: Une lecture de 'la secte du Phoenix' de Jorge Luis Borges," in *Revue de Psychanalyse* 70 (April 2000).

17. Cathy Caruth, *Literature in the Ashes of History* (Baltimore: Johns Hopkins University Press, 2013), 6.

18. Walter Benjamin, "Theses on the Philosophy of History," in *Illuminations*, ed. Hannah Arendt, trans. Harry Zohn (New York: Harcourt, Brace & World, 1968), 257–258.

Chapter Four

Austrißized

Woman in Gold

Gustav Klimt's painting was originally titled *The Portrait of Adele Bloch-Bauer* but was changed by the Nazis to "*Dame en Or*," which translates in English to "*Woman in Gold*." It is not only paradigmatic of his *oeuvre*; it depicts a feminine *jouissance* that exceeds meaning and representation.[1] Klimt spearheaded an artistic revolution that reinvented femininity and aimed, as part of the modernist project, to depict the unrepresentable—that is, *jouissance*. In this sense, *Woman in Gold* is a painting subject to a long story of appropriation as both placeless and stateless. As leader of the Secession movement, Klimt's *oeuvre* begins precisely where Freud's met an impasse, namely with the question "What does a woman want?"

The fin-de-siècle painter's work prefigures Lacan's later elaboration of feminine *jouissance*, frustrating meaning, nationhood, borders, ownership, and even changing what it means to see. Simon Curtis's film *Woman in Gold* (2015)[2] rekindles attention to Klimt's painting, in particular *Woman in Gold*, which raises questions of belonging with regard to art and *jouissance*. Portraying an Otherness to representation, *Woman in Gold* presents an *unheimlich* account that ideologies of diversity and multiculturalism cannot begin to fathom let alone accommodate.

Klimt's presentation of feminine *jouissance* in this portrait invites us to reconsider ideas of belonging and the extinguished women in his works. The saga of *Woman in Gold* unmasks the hypocrisy of Holocaust "acquisitions," the arbitrary value of the art market, and even the troublesome business of postwar reparations. While many of Klimt's paintings were destroyed by the Nazis, *The Portrait of Adele Bloch-Bauer* survived as a reminder of the genocide and the destruction of the well-to-do Viennese Jewish community, and as an uncanny remainder of their property and person. The painting, like Adele Bloch-Bauer herself, has become a symbol of the impossible wished-for restitution. Its return to the descendants is not an example of consolatory compensation or comforting closure for Holocaust victims, but a reminder of irreparable loss. Instead it persists as a souvenir and symbol of the perpetual exile of Adele Bauer and her family, the painting, Klimt's revolutionary art, and feminine *jouissance*.

The logic of restitution concerns the act of restoring an object that was lost, stolen, or unjustly declared state property to its rightful owner. The word "restitution" is composed of the words "rest" and "it." As a figure of *jouissance*, or what Freud initially called the "Id," Klimt's portrait is something that can never rest or be brought "home." In fact, in a Freudian *Weltanschauung*, such *jouissance* problematizes any notion of home (*heim*). It is precisely what the "home" must repress in order to be a home. The return of the painting to the family's descendants is thus *not* a restoration; the law cannot re-establish, rectify, or make up for the destitution and theft. Rather, it creates a fiction of justice or a kind of false equivalency as though some form of reparation could be made. Restitution is a fiction that drives the film, *Woman in Gold*, as a symptom of capitalism and its discontents.

The film *Woman in Gold* (2015) is based on the book titled *Lady in Gold: The Extraordinary Tale of Gustav Klimt's Masterpiece, Portrait of Adele Bloch-Bauer* by Anne Marie O'Connor and tells the story of this pilfered and itinerant painting.[3] Both the book and the film narrate the Bloch-Bauer saga through the painting's beneficiary, Maria Altmann. The book includes elements not mentioned in the film, such as Adele's amorous relationship with Klimt, her early death by typhoid, and the Bloch-Bauers' descent and ultimate deportation under Nazi occupation, including the extent and cost of the trials for the painting's repatriation.

Yet, the film does not show some key aspects of the story, such as how only a few members of the Bloch-Bauer family, including Maria Altmann, a young newlywed at the time, were able to escape through extraordinary bribes and the help of a Dutch pastor.[4] The Bloch-Bauers, like Klimt's other wealthy Viennese patrons, had their property seized, and many were murdered by the Nazis. Glossing and selectively omitting, the film focuses on Maria's attempts at restitution as a refugee in the United States and the drawn-out court battles. Thus, as a commodity itself concerned with box office sales, the film elides more problematic aspects of the novel and the historical events that inspired it. For example, the film only briefly alludes to the fact that Adele's husband was sent to Dachau and that Nazis killed the rest of her family. We see this in flashbacks that remain narratively undeveloped.[5]

While the film includes some past scenes that show Adele as a younger woman posing for Klimt, it also curiously neglects the fact that she was

Klimt's mistress, a powerful salon presence, a socialite, and a communist in a politically volatile fin-de-siècle Vienna. The film emphasizes her disempowerment rather than her complex political and social power, including how she was a champion of "Red Vienna," espousing feminist and communist causes. The film soft-pedals these sympathies, aspects of her character that would have given an American film audience pause.

The fiction that "ownership" can be restored or reestablished is buttressed by the film's story of a necklace handed down from Adele to Maria, which was invented solely with narrative closure for the audience in mind. In a flashback scene, Adele, the socialite at the height of her power, gives her young niece Maria (played by Helen Mirren) the necklace. While most people do not have a world historical painting in their family's past, they might well have a necklace. This scene connects the audience, the painting, the feminine, and the family jewels in a more recognizable fashion and makes the viewer feel a solid link between Maria and her aunt, further supporting the comforting fiction of ownership. Here, the film's sugarcoating illustrates our point: belonging is imaginary, and the symbolic order upholds ideologies of group belonging. The real story of the painting and the family is the history of the Holocaust: the fact that human beings can be stripped of all ownership and belonging, reduced to flesh for the fire.

Before she died in 1923, Adele left a short will expressing her wish that her jewelry be inherited by Gustav Bloch-Bauer's daughters, Luise and Maria, and her Klimt paintings be donated to the Belvedere Gallery in Vienna.[6] Since Adele was unable to bear children, ultimately her sister Maria and then her cousins were made the beneficiaries of her estate. In actuality, Adele's necklace, which is in the portrait, was used as collateral for the family to escape Vienna before the *Anschluss*. After the *Anschluss*, Adele's wishes were not executed, and the family Klimt paintings were absconded with by Nazi art looting. This pillaging continued even after the war when Adele's husband Ferdinand further relinquished family paintings to the Austrian gallery in negotiations, despite the fact that Luise and Maria were named as beneficiaries.[7] Basically, the Austrian government continued even after the war to profit from negotiations with Jewish exiles and survivors when they tried to reclaim their possessions. After negotiations, the Bloch-Bauer Klimt paintings were obtained by the Belvedere museum. Hence, Adele's original wishes were never fulfilled and the portrait remained a curious testament, questioning the very ideology of ownership that it would be used to support.

Both the film and the painting memorialize previously erased events, including Adele's name, which was quickly stripped from the painting after the Nazi seizure. O'Connor explains, "The wealthy muse of Klimt, his patron, his friend, and perhaps much more, was wiped away. Adele Bloch-Bauer was now simply the '*Lady in Gold*.'"[8] After the war, the Nazis gave Klimt's portrait its new title: *Dame in Geld*. While the situations are not equivalent, Adele, like *Woman in Berlin*'s Anonyma, is stripped of her name even after restitution is supposedly accomplished, thus revealing the erasure of both German and Jewish plundered women.

The film is structured around the court case, which is meant to remedy this erasure and restore the woman's name to the painting, and the painting to her family. The omission of the name is the Nazis' attempt to wipe out the Jewish "taint" in Klimt's paintings—not only the Jewish women who sat for him, but also the depiction of feminine *jouissance* he practiced and attempted to represent in his art. While it was easy for the Nazis to erase the "Jewish stain" in Klimt's art by killing off his models, it was harder to erase their radiant visages in Klimt's paintings, a testament to feminine *jouissance*.

The Nazis alternately viewed Klimt's paintings on the one hand as fin-de-siècle masterpieces, and as worthless decadent "shit" on the other. The metamorphosis from shit to gold is what Freud described as sublimation or the movement in anal eroticism from feces as gift to cultural object. Klimt's art exposed the arbitrariness of the Nazis anointing and deposing value on objects. The painting foregrounds a material real that resists objectification—for example, the price tag of the *Reichstag*. In actuality, Klimt's paintings embody pricelessness and placelessness, or provide a home in the diaspora that is art.

Part of Klimt's artistic revolution is that a material real in his paintings, *jouissance*, is able to put symbolic and cultural values into question. One way the painter does this is through the incorporation of real gold into his work. Klimt's practice is an intentional resistance to normativity with regard to monetary value. The painter grew up poor; his father was a gold-engraver. Bullion symbolized everything that was out of reach for Klimt's family.[9] Spreading gold on a canvas was a way of reconceiving and repositioning value, not only for himself, but on behalf of a cosmopolitan Viennese moneyed public. Klimt's paintings provide a critical perspective on the arbitrariness of wealth that prefigures modernism and the explosion of new markets as a result of technology and the ensuing world wars.

All the models featured in Klimt's paintings, including Adele Bloch-Bauer, were simultaneously portrayed as desiring but also as women of symbolic and cultural wealth. They are depicted in the very same way that real gold is used. The Bloch-Bauers, like the Mahlers, the Rothschilds, or the Lederers, amassed fabulous riches through banking and commodities. Like the gold standard, which is now defunct, the Nazis attempted to abolish the subject matter of Klimt's paintings and the "value" of Jewish ownership itself. Today the gold in Klimt's work reminds us of a lost or "old" culture—that is, Jewish Viennese society before the *Anschluss*. A relic of that gold, that precious *jouissance*, remains on display in Klimt's paintings.

Wealthy Viennese families, like the Bloch-Bauers, had no trouble parting with fabulous riches and whatever was demanded of them to avoid the camps. When the Bloch-Bauer family left, they sold everything to save their lives. As exiles stripped of ownership and symbolic position, wealthy Viennese Jews were not only divided subjects, but doubly displaced in what we are calling a double barring of subjectivity: $. Instead of Lacan's barred subject with one slash through the *S*, we use the dollar sign, with two slashes through the *S* to designate this erasure. This dollar sign symbolizes how value in the symbolic and the ability to participate in the dignity of meaning was destroyed. The fates of many of the actual women painted in Klimt's works were exemplary of such a double-barred subjectivity. They were completely stripped, not only of their family treasures, but of subjectivity itself. This can be compared to what Agamben calls bare life, existence at the limit of the human, *Homo Sacer*.

For Lacan, a capital *S* with a line dividing the letter is the matheme of the barred subject. It is a matheme that shows that a subject is divided by language, and that *jouissance*, denoted by the letter *a* is tethered to another place. The formula is written *S* barred *poincon* object *a*. Discourse bars *jouissance* and creates meaning and community. Lacan's barred subject is determined by the unconscious. The bar denotes repression and cultural inclusion through barred *jouissance*. It is worth remarking that the double bar is the sign for the dollar, as Lacan explains in the discourse of the capitalist.[10] Capitalism does not separate the subject from *jouissance*, as the law had previously done, making discourse possible, but commands us to enjoy. The "double barred" dollar can be thought of as the "subject" under late capitalism who is further reduced to raw material for corporate enjoyment and appropriated by dominant ideology—that is, "*Just do it!*"

As *The Portrait of Adele Bloch-Bauer* reveals, the designation of value of art objects has become more and more arbitrary under advanced capitalism. This is shown in the 2006 Lauder purchase of the Klimt *Portrait of Adele Bloch-Bauer* for $135 million, "the highest sum ever paid for a painting" at the time.[11] In a contemporary reality show of Poe's "Oval Portrait," the art object that is *Portrait of Adele Bloch Bauer* has become more valuable than the actual woman's life. When the painting left Vienna and was being transported to America, many Austrians put posters with "*adieu*" in the streets, bidding the painting goodbye.[12] Where were they when the Viennese Jews were being taken to the camps? The Viennese reserved their meaning only for their Viennese *Mona Lisa*.

Yet, the art object, like Adele herself, was no more at home in Vienna than with Maria Altmann after the court case. Klimt's painting demonstrates the unbelonging of the work of art, which, like femininity, can never be owned or fully "housed" in any place. The court's decision to return the painting to Maria also reveals the inability of law to arbitrate human loss. The value of art is closest to the dead woman in that it is similarly an object that cannot belong and resists the restoration of value. It is the only thing of the woman that lives on *after death*.

Even though restitution isn't accomplished and the painting never goes home, "home" as a relation of past and present is made possible through the association of Maria Altmann and Randy Schoenberg, her lawyer. Randy is the grandson of composer Arnold Schoenberg, known for inventing twelve-tone music. This renewed family connection transforms tragedy into history. It is not a restoration of family but a construction that allows historic testimony. On a social level, the court case helped Randy Schoenberg with his own career, his relation to his wife, and his relation to the past and his family name. Initially, Schoenberg didn't want to defend the case and experienced ambivalence about digging into the traumatic past. The film's story renders him the good grandson of Arnold Schoenberg who now has a meaningful relation to his past that is no longer forgotten.

Randy's change of mind occurs when his enthusiasm shifts after the voyage to Austria with Maria Altmann. In Vienna, both the trial and the city's memorials—for example, the Holocaust Memorial—begin to make Schoenberg feel reconnected by way of strolling around. As he experiences the recalcitrance of the Austrian art world and government in court, he becomes emboldened in the legal battle. Contrarily, Maria, who is in her eighties, becomes more beaten down as the case proceeds. The Austrian gallery lawyer hopes to run the clock out on the plaintiff in the case.

This is similar to the way Vienna used the process of "*tauschhandel*" to barter or bicker over survivors' stolen property, thus continuing to profit off Nazi pilfered goods,[13] as we mentioned earlier regarding Ferdinand Bloch-Bauer. Even after the war, Vienna made surviving Jews fill out "export permits" to donate or trade valuable artworks to receive their property back. This type of bargaining was widespread, as alluded to but also whitewashed in the film *Monuments Men* when Roosevelt's Monuments Men returned looted art to Germany after World War II.[14] While the Germans were supposed to return the art to the victims' families, they more often returned Nazi-looted artwork to the very high-ranking Nazis who stole them.[15] Neither film fully reveals the duplicity of the establishment Vienna art market. *Woman in Gold* also shows how the gallery lawyers preferred to deal with Randy, who was of the younger generation and not a direct survivor, carrying the weight of memory and history.

Austrian journalist Hubertus Czernin helped Schoenberg and Altmann win the Klimt case by unearthing Adele's will. He believed the lawsuit was not only a battle between Jew and Gentile, but an international debate about war crimes and reparations (Reed). It brings up the idea that restitutions of art can never serve as a replacement for the destruction and damages of war. Destruction relates to *jouissance* as part of Freud's death drive, but also to *eros*, a creative life force. Hence sublimated objects, such as Klimt's paintings and other artworks, remain as unique relics and historical reminders that live on after death.

As another example of art that testifies to the obliteration of Jewish fin-de-siècle culture, Felix Salten's *Bambie: Eine Lebensgeschichte aus dem Walde* (1923) was written at the same historical moment as *The Portrait of Adele Bloch Bauer* was painted. Hitler banned both these works before they became cultural icons. Salten's *Bambi*, like his *Josephine Mutzenbacher: The Life Story of a Viennese Whore, as Told by Herself*,[16] is about a confrontation with feminine *jouissance* as unruly wild, scary, and vulnerable. Salten, like *other* prominent Viennese Jews, fled Austria to Switzerland and barely avoided death in the camps. His novel *Bambi* now lives on as a powerful political allegory on the mistreatment of Jews.[17] Despite all the attempts to obliterate Vienna's fin-de-siècle culture, these artworks remain as witnesses.

The Portrait of Adele Bloch-Bauer shows how the artwork, like feminine *jouissance*, remains atemporal and uncanny, but for this very reason, allows for a Sinthomatic construction of history. Adele, like Maria Altmann and Randy Schoenberg, ultimately ends up in America, which is home to refugees, immigrants, and those who have been exiled or had to leave their homes. Klimt's *Portrait of Adele Bloch-Bauer* remains a reminder of loss, a souvenir of what was destroyed. Simon Curtis's film domesticates the itinerant and placeless *jouissance* in Klimt's painting, the way the Nazis tried to tame Klimt's work and the way the Austrians made it their very own masterpiece. None of these attempts to diminish the painting's power by ownership were successful. While the death of Adele and Viennese fin-de-siècle culture were catastrophic, the artwork remains a testament to a person and place that no longer exists. Tourists flock to the portrait that hangs today in the Neue Galerie in order to ponder the mysterious story behind one of the costliest acquisitions in art history. "Who knows why it cost so much?" an onlooker asked her partner when one of the authors of this chapter recently visited the museum. The mystery of the painting's value remains its most treasured gift.

NOTES

1. Gustav Klimt, *Portrait of Adele Bloch-Bauer I: The Woman in Gold*, 1907, oil, silver, and gold on canvas, 54 x 54 in., 1907, Neue Gallerie, https://www.neuegalerie.org/content/gustav-klimt-and-adele-bloch-bauer-woman-gold.
2. Simon Curtis, dir., *Woman in Gold*, 2015.
3. Anne Marie O'Connor, *The Lady in Gold: The Extraordinary Tale of Gustav Klimt's Masterpiece, "Portrait of Adele Bloch-Bauer"* (New York: Vintage, 2015).
4. O'Connor, *The Lady in Gold*, 132.
5. O'Connor, *The Lady in Gold*, 124.
6. O'Connor, *The Lady in Gold*, 68. Also, Hubertus Czernin, a Viennese journalist, uncovered crucial documents for the case in 1998, including the details of her will. See Christopher Reed, "Hubertus Czernin," *The Guardian*, July 3, 2006, https://www.theguardian.com/news/2006/jul/04/guardianobituaries.austria.

7. O'Connor, *The Lady in Gold*, 199.
8. O'Connor, *The Lady in Gold*, 152.
9. O'Connor, *The Lady in Gold*, 17.
10. Jacques Lacan, "On Psychoanalytic Discourse: The Milan Lecture," trans. Jack Stone, *La Salmandra* (1978): 10–11; and Lacan, *The Other Side of Psychoanalysis*, trans. Jacques-Alain Miller, vol. 17, *The Seminar of Jacques Lacan, XVII* (New York: W. W. Norton, 2007) describes capitalist discourse as a substitute for the master discourse. These works explain how the "subject" under capitalism has become a slave to *jouissance* and the fodder of super egoic demands. Fascist Germany, like late capital, involves a market structured by *jouissance* and not the Names of the Father.
11. Carol Vogel, "Lauder Pays $135 Million, a Record, for a Klimt Portrait," *The New York Times*, June 19, 2006.
12. O'Connor, *The Lady in Gold*, 255.
13. Terrence Turner, dir., *Adele's Wish*, 2008, is an in-depth account of Maria Altmann's court case and issues with the republic of Austria, including "*Tauschhandel*."
14. George Clooney, dir., *The Monuments Men*, 2014.
15. "Hili Perlson, "Bavaria Kept Nazi-Looted Art in Museums," artnet News, June 28, 2016, https://news.artnet.com/art-world/germany-returned-nazi-looted-art-nazi-families-530786.
16. Originally published as Josefine Mutzenbacher, *Josefine Mutzenbacher oder Die Geschichte einer Wienerischen Dirne von ihr selbst erzählt.* (Erscheinungsort nicht ermittelbar: Verlag nicht ermittelbar, 1906). Felix Salten is now widely acknowledged to be the author, though it was published anonymously and he never claimed authorship. It has been republished as Felix Salten and Marix Verlag, *Bambi: Eine Lebensgeschichte aus dem Walde* (Wiesbaden, Germany: Verlagshaus, 2016). Finally, see Kelsey Osgood, "Before Bambi, There Was Josephine: Felix Salten's Erotic Literature," *The American Reader*, accessed August 22, 2018, http://theamericanreader.com/before-bambi-there-was-josefine/.
17. O'Connor, *The Lady in Gold*, 100.

Chapter Five

Music as the Last Word

The Lives of Others

Florian Henckel von Donnersmarck's *The Lives of Others* (*Das Leben der Anderen*) (2006) demonstrates how art can interrupt a subject laboring under a totalitarian fantasy, ideology, and control.[1] Gerd Wiesler, the Stasi officer, becomes less Communist after hearing the score "Sonata for a Good Man," written especially for the film by Gabriel Yared.[2] When Wiesler listens to the music while spying on the GDR playwright Georg Dreyman, it makes him anxiously question Stasi principles. Likewise, the film displays the destitution of identifying with a group fantasy. The sonata facilitates artistic engagement for those who listen that initiates questions about state control. In *The Lives of Others*, what subverts a totalitarian fantasy is not the sonata or art in itself, but how it is engaged.

The Lebanese-born musician Gabriel Yared specifically composed "Sonata for a Good Man" for the film. Donnersmarck and Yared worked together to conceive the score as a musical cross between the sound of Claude Lanzmann's Nazi documentary *Shoah* and *The Talented Mr. Ripley*.[3] As more inventive than representative, *The Lives of Others* is about those "Others" subjected to surveillance, psychological torture, and banishment from legal history in postwar Berlin. Not only is the film a portrayal of washed-out East German officials—as the Stasi officer Gerd Wiesler proclaims, "*Es ist für mich*"—it also relates to all citizens that have become refugees, exiles, or excised from history: "*Es ist für uns*."

In his critique of the film, Slavoj Žižek says that *The Lives of Others* is not historically accurate and "misses the true horror" of the GDR. It is true that the film contains interactions between the artist and Stasi officer that most likely did not occur and, as Žižek claims, that "in this way the horror that was inscribed into the very structure of the East German system is relegated to a mere personal whim."[4] Indeed, the film does not provide a complete representation of GDR terror. Yet how could any film do so without being completely tedious or unendurably *langweilig* (*Shoah*). Indeed, the film is most engaging for its non-representational aspects. The film's significance comes from its aural and circulatory notes, which make a supplemental cinematic archive to history. Its cinematic significance comes from the "Sonata for a Good Man," which punctuates, as Paul Celan writes in his poem "Death Fugue," "death's music / death / comes as a master from Germany."[5] The film and its sonata set off an ethical search for the real story beyond the officially documented Stasi reality.

Supporting Žižek's comments, the film does not depict the GDR realistically, but it does indirectly present GDR atrocities, like suicide, as tied to the disruption of artistic invention. The Stasi punishes Albert Jerska, a banned playwright and director who commits suicide, thoroughly for his anti-state theater.[6] In contrast, the main characters are not radically threatened by the state. Sidelined or supplemental characters such as Jerska and Christa-Maria suffer rape, exile, and banishment in the former GDR. Both end up committing suicide and suffer for their cynicism of Stasi rule. Indeed, the main characters that Žižek mentions are unbelievable—Georg Dreyman and Gerd Wiesler—and not as ethically engaged as Jerska or Christa-Maria, but they soften the blow of the other artists who disrupt Stasi state control through aesthetic invention, which leads to their suicide or worse. Hence, resistance comes through the Other as an interruptive aesthetic exposure, more so than the characters or plot of the film.

Going in and outside the filmic frame, "Sonata for a Good Man" significantly relates to the characters' questioning of totalitarianism and Stasi decline. The sonata is a posthumous gift from Jerska to Georg Dreyman. As Dreyman listens to the music, it inadvertently and circuitously affects the observant Wiesler. When Jerska gives the "Sonata for a Good Man" to Dreyman, it is the artist's fortieth birthday, a gift between artists. Fearing a fate similar to his friend, Dreyman doesn't start playing it until after Jerska's death when he starts writing again himself. As he listens, Dreyman is inspired and wonders how anyone who hears it could fail to be affected. Unbeknownst to him, Gerd Wiesler, the Stasi officer listening upstairs, is affected and sits crying in a rare display of emotion.

After listening to the sonata, the Stasi officer becomes sympathetic to the artists he is watching: the writer Georg Dreyman and his actress girlfriend, Christa-Maria Sieland. The hidden "Other" no longer views the artist as the Other he is watching or an object of surveillance, but as an interesting person. As a hidden listener in the attic, Gerd Wiesler becomes "curiously enchanted with what he hears through his headphones, connected to the bugs concealed behind the wallpaper of the playwright's apartment: that rich world of literature, music, friendship, and tender sex [is] so different from his own desiccated solitary life in a dreary tower-block."[7] After listening to the sonata, Wiesler begins to violate all the rules that he had learned and was taught at the Stasi academy. In a pathetic attempt to mirror the vivacity and intimacy he has witnessed, he hires a revolting prostitute and starts reading Bertolt Brecht.

While the sonata makes Wiesler anxiously question his belief in the totalitarian state, it doesn't make him "good," but it allows him to allow others to be good. Indeed, it is unlikely that an officer like Wiesler existed or would have been recorded as existing. If a GDR bureaucrat aided or even sympathized with a suspect, they would likely be removed from history. *The Lives of Others*' decision to invent Wiesler is more poetic and mythic than representative. It is a cinematic revisioning of postwar Berlin and the possibility of unrecorded accounts.

In an NPR interview, Donnersmarck relates Wiesler's turn from being Stasi to the "Sonata for a Good Man" as a force of aesthetic engagement. He notes how Lenin confessed that he might not have been able to finish the Soviet revolution had he really listened to Beethoven's *Appassionata*.[8] *The Lives of Others* testifies to Lenin's allegation regarding the powerful role of art for subverting a totalitarian ideology. While the "Sonata for a Good Man" does not keep Wiesler from committing GDR atrocities, it does make him question his collaboration with, and belief in, Stasi rhetoric. Moreover, the sonata facilitates an uncoming engagement that undermines his identification with the state.

The sonata changes Gerd Wiesler in an inexplicable way that is not reducible to any symbolic or representational identification. As it echoes through the ceiling, Wiesler begins to realize the intimacy of identifying with the Other and becomes less engaged in his own grim reality. As a vicarious gift, the sonata allows Wiesler to be released from ego imprisonment, if only for a moment, even though it was originally meant for Dreyman. The sonata, like Beethoven's *Appassionata*, is not owned by anyone—even its composer Yared. It is written to engage the filmic audience, as well as the Stasi officer. It imagines an impossible situation—Lenin or Wiesler hearing music that would hinder or break through their imaginary ideological imprisonment. Thus, the sonata resonates for all those uncoming others engaged in a participatory bond beside a mimetic state apparatus based on belonging.

The enigmatic and engaging quality of "otherness" in Yared's sonata relates to what Jacques Lacan calls the acoustic object that brings up anxiety.[9] In passive artistic engagements, this anxiety is stopped by fantasy and with object *a*. Contrarily, a more active engagement hears this acoustic opening in the symbolic not as a sublime uplift but as a mysterious "fall," causing the listener, through anxiety, to engage.[10] *The Lives of Others* is not an homage to Yared, Lenin, or Beethoven, but an imagined hypothetical participation in an uncoming community outside militant representation. In this sense, the film shows how a measure of anxiety can facilitate aesthetic reinvention. With the sonata, Wiesler allows himself a measure of not knowing or private enjoyment, which, until this music, his Stasi identification had not allowed.

Despite its romanticizing of the GDR, *The Lives of Others* still displays a potentially disruptive mode of aesthetic engagement for those suffering under a totalitarian rule. Yared's score is a psychological piece that uses no words and works without acoustic explanation. Donnersmarck and Yared collaborated to come up with a classical and contemporary score that does not easily fit into any aesthetic or filmic category. Indeed, when Yared first presented it to Donnersmarck, the director initially found it too difficult. Then, after finding no other score, he became convinced of its "otherness" and mystifying qualities. "Sonata for a Good Man" is not just a part of the plot or limited to the action in *The Lives of Others*; it uncannily goes in and out of the representation, resisting the filmic frame.[11] The sonata works as an uncanny force that defies East German Stasi limits, unlawfully and freely moving both within and outside all the different segmented parts of the city and its interned citizens.

The film uses music to evoke what Jacques Lacan in *Seminar VII* calls an ethical sublime beyond any symbolic or group identification. Jerska's "Sonata for a Good Man" is his last composition, a grand finale, a *nachlass* or death note that inadvertently initiates an "ethical" reaction in Wiesler. Ethics, as defined by Lacan, is a turn away from the state and "the morality of the master, created for the virtues of the master and linked to the order of powers."[12] It goes beyond the social good, into desire, or what we can do, or are able to do insofar as it is impossible, not what we are "supposed to do."[13] The ethical is the impossible, an act that defies the symbolic order of objects, goods, teleology, and ideology as closure. As Jerska's work does not represent the "good" of the state, it is an ethical score that resists totalitarian control. He engages in the impossible by way of his sonata and legacy, a traitorous act. Jerska's *nachlaß* is *The Lives of Others* revisioning through a musical score; "The Sonata for a Good Man" refuses representational frames by offering an ongoing aesthetic and ethical engagement for the other/audience.

While most people use fantasy to cover over the sublime, *The Lives of Others* shows real lies in group identifications that are enforced through belonging. As an ethical figure, Jerska's "fall"—that is, suicide—means he doesn't even fit into the art world or existence itself. He gives the sonata to Dreyman in what Gerard Wajcman calls a "desublimating act."[14] As a suicidal send-off, Jerska's sonata challenges absolutism literally head-on when he "falls" or jump through the window of fantasy.[15] Thus Jerska's rejection of Stasi ideology is a jump into an annihilating real. While the playwright doesn't survive, the Sonata lives on as a Sinthomatic engagement affecting not only the characters of Gerd Wiesler and Georg Dreyman, but also those who watch, the filmic audience itself.

In the film, Gerd Wiesler ends up as the "good" Stasi officer who turns from totalitarianism through a perverse fantasy involving the GDR artists. When he hears the sonata it destabilizes but does not destroy his allegiance to the state. His voyeurism temporarily lifts, propelling him into action instead of waiting for validation from an authoritarian Other. He realizes that a life of principled devotion is missing something. Wiesler's turn from Stasi recognition is not conveyed in words but in his changing relation to the lives of those he watches—that is, the Others. After listening to the music, Wiesler identifies with Others and desires to be part of their uncoming community.

Ulrich Mühe plays Wiesler as a largely silent figure whose compelling facial expressions convey the character change, including a tear upon hearing the sonata. Indeed, at first Wiesler appears dead but comes alive when he begins to realize himself as something *other* than Stasi. In protecting the artists, Wiesler becomes more engaged and less identified with the state. Then he begins to write a Stasi "report" that is not purely accurate and displays his own creative side. Wiesler doesn't actually record the "facts" on Dreyman, but composes fiction with his account.

Gerd Wiesler's "turn" from an accurate archive and rejection of GDR ideology allegorically relates to the East German turn (*die Wende*) when the Berlin Wall fell (*der Mauerfall*). The country and the system remained intact, but citizens were incalculably affected by the fall of GDR ideology. They could no longer rely on group identifications of Stasi or the East German state, which were shattered and stripped of value. Ironically, this was the beginning of a Berlin revisioning; the city became a cosmopolitan mecca of artists and Others.

In history *die Wende* means "the change" or the turning point that made East Germany into something Other. Since November 9, 1989, it has been possible to own property there and to engage in many formerly prohibited activities. Whether this is "a change for the better" (*eine Wende zum Besseren*) is the big question of reunification (*die Wiedervereinigung*), a word that is now synonymous with all of those events. Since the reunification (*Seit der Wende*) or "the fall of the Wall"—the "turn" toward Otherness has been sometimes optimistic, overlooking the gaps or mistakes in East German archives.[16] *The Lives of Others* steps in this gap to imagine the Stasi officer or citizen after *die Wende*. It does not imagine culture through reunification or restitution but through music and Sinthomatic invention.

Germany, as Timothy Garton Ash notes, is a world master in the production of cruel dictatorships. Yet it has also become better at engaging in a cultural revisioning of itself as Other. *The Lives of Others* opens in 1984, not to remember Orwell, but Chernyenko, the very Communist Russian president who preceded Gorbachev.[17] The film begins in an "anywhere" environment without title or name, to convey a common political mistake that culminated in Chernyenko's rule. As some of the only words on its screen, the film's beginning projects the Stasi said goal, of "knowing everything." Instead, the film affirms aesthetic engagement and empathy with "Otherness" to avoid totalitarian representation.

The Stasi paranoid project is neither history nor simply an East German (GDR) problem but relates to any paranoid initiative of state control. In the United States today, our own intelligence community similarly aims for "total information awareness" through absolute military control and surveillance. Indeed, its political aim to "know everything" is a failed historic project not limited to East Germany and is a feature of the American Patriot Act. Another example is the Google Maps project, which was adapted from Keyhole satellites, built with CIA investment. There are secret police in America who, like the Stasi, see without being seen, clandestinely incarcerate, and obliterate privacy.

At the film's turning point, Gerd Wiesler—the devoted Stasi—begins to realize the futility of absolute "knowledge." He starts writing fiction into his archive to recover a real lack or the privacy of not being recognized by the authoritarian state. He ends every entry with his identifier, HGW XX/7, in red, which Dreyman later uses to identify the author, i.e., error (lack) of this Stasi officer who inadvertently helped him publish.

At the end of the film, Georg Dreyman goes back to the records and realizes the "truth" in Wiesler's fiction. Dreyman was both under surveillance and protected by the Stasi, which didn't stop the suicide of his beloved Christa-Maria. Indeed, as he reads Wiesler's archive, it conveys a fictional truth beyond the facts. Thus, the records Wiesler keeps, like "Sonata for a Good Man," testify to what's left out of "objective" history.

Working through supplemental notes not reducible to Stasi categories, *The Lives of Others* displays an "Other" account that never existed in official records. This uncanny testimony of the film is the "place of consignation, [indicated] with a technique of repetition, and without a certain exteriority. No archive without outside."[18] When Gerd becomes engaged in fixing the records, he writes about events beyond Stasi orchestration. The word "archive" comes from the Greek and means "*arkheion*: initially a house, domicile, an address, the residence of the superior magistrates, the archons, those who commanded."[19] By incorporating an exterior fictional element into the archive, Wiesler makes a home for himself and the artists he observes. Likewise, *The Lives of Others* uses aesthetic engagement to imagine East German citizens that participate as "Other" in an uncoming community beside group identification.

Many critics and photographers, like Harald Houswald, remind us that photography and film were censored in the GDR by the state. *The Lives of*

Others would not even have been made in East Germany, where the quality and color of film was very bad. In keeping with the reality of the GDR, Donnersmarck decided not to include too much red or blue since these were uncommon colors and not "authentic" during the time period. The film replaces red with a brownish-orange and blue with green or gray, for the most part, except for the manuscripts. It is significant when Dreyman, like Wiesler, uses red ink and it bleeds all over his hands while writing an article on suicide for *Der Spiegel*. The red ink indicates a non-representational aspect of the film that conveys a hidden truth: The GDR didn't simply censor film, photography, and color—they grossly underestimated and misrepresented the color of life, including the darkness of suicide. In this sense, Dreyman's fictional article is more a revisioning than an "objective" record.

According to Heidegger's essay on the "Origin of the Work of Art," truth is what the artwork gives in its relation to *aletheia*.[20] The red ink is what Dreyman uses to write; like the sonata that came from Jerska's blood, it is the way he lives on. It is an acoustic object that causes anxiety and a trace of the uncanny that is denied or repressed by official channels. Donnersmarck incorporates the historically incorrect red stain to present a real, atrocious aspect of East German life—that is, the suicides that were stricken from the records in Stasi Germany.

Dreyman's article is written on a smuggled typewriter that is brought in to avoid typeface identification. Also, he uses a pseudonym to discuss statistics banned from the "official" Stasi storyline. All this encoding is required since the GDR repressed and prohibited "stats" on suicide. Dreyman challenges the "official" notion that only crazy artists and individuals commit suicide.[21] Indeed, these deaths say less about the individual than the societal madness of a totalitarian rule that weighed so heavily on so many citizens who took their own lives. While the state claims to "know everything," death marks a place where it stops counting. The film shows how these suicides mark an exception to the totalitarian rule of "knowing everything." Indeed, the Stasi could not predict or control suicide, revealing the impotence of an absolutist regime over death and the drives. As falling into this place of exception, Christa-Maria and Jerska exercise free will beyond state control, and their suicide is the subtext and inspiration for Dreyman's article.

Working through "Sonata for a Good Man," the film makes an ahistorical and ethical act that results from aesthetic engagement. This type of ethics is not found in representational depictions of Communist East Germany. Ash quotes Donnersmarck, saying that "in a movie the reality is always to be *verdichtet*, a word which means thickened, concentrated, intensified, but carries a verbal association with *Dichtung*, meaning poetry, or more broadly fiction."[22] Instead of trying to be representational, *The Lives of Others* works through *Dichtung*, or the poetic story of the sonata and a truth (*aletheia*) that is Other than the symbolic archive.

In another play on the real, Donnersmarck describes his discussions with Stasi officers about "odor samples," which were taken by German bureaucrats who left swaths across chairs to capture the scent of citizens' genitalia. These swatches were then submitted to dogs for the purposes of future identification. While seemingly crass and surreal, this process indeed happened in real life, and the director didn't make it an obvious part of the film. In many scenes, the characters are paranoid about sitting down, as in the horrible scene where Christa-Maria is asked to sit before being blackmailed to reveal information about Dreyman. The film plays with the smelly reality of East Germany that seems unreal since it was repressed by a totalitarian rule. The odor samples were a technique for the Stasi to reject those it considered trash and who did not serve any symbolic "good."[23] In alluding to the GDR's attempt to sanitize humanity, Donnersmarck's film presents an abject real more than reality. *The Lives of Others* conveys the "dross" of sanitized GDR history as an acoustic "Other" archive.[24]

Thus, realistic presentations only symbolize the individual suffering and sometimes prop up a totalitarian fantasy. Contrarily, *The Lives of Others* facilitates an aesthetic engagement that questions authoritarian and representational rule. However, the use of art does not de facto overturn an imprisoning ideology, as mentioned by George Steiner in relation to Nazi Germany: "We know that a man can read Goethe or Rilke in the evening, or that he can play Bach and Schubert, and then go to his day's work at Auschwitz in the morning."[25] Indeed, it is not the music as object that is ineffective, but the way a jaded bureaucrat engages the aesthetic to prop up his narcissism.

If the music is "other," it may temporarily stop us from our egomaniacal identifications. Unlike Steiner's Nazi officer, Gerd Wiesler begins to engage music as "Other" to question a totalitarian fantasy. *The Lives of Others* counters the idea that art should serve as a symbolic good to emphasize its force as an uncontrolled engagement with "Others."

Abject characters are most difficult for a totalitarian state to utilize, as is the case with Christa-Maria, who is obsessively chased and punished by the Stasi Minister Hempf. In contrast to Wiesler, Hempf holds enough power to gratify his base desires and exploit the system. Still, Hempf is racked by this woman whom he cannot control and, instead of admitting weakness, attempts to eliminate the object that limits his absolute power. Indeed, Steiner's mythical Nazi officer who goes back to killing after listening to beautiful music is shown to be Hempf's predecessor. He neither sees nor hears any other and goes on with his blind and bland life of subservience to the Other. Contrarily, Christa-Maria and other artists, such as Jerska, suffer from his inhumane, absolutist engagement.

Most of the characters, including Dreyman, do not understand just how deeply Christa-Maria has been abjected by the GDR system. Still, Dreyman's radical friends do not trust her, as they are familiar with the danger of becoming the "dross" in Stasi history. She is also completely misunderstood by Wiesler, for whom femininity is a total anathema. In a bar scene where Wiesler is trying to control events with his "fiction," he tells Christa-Maria he is a fan and persuades her to go home to Dreyman instead of Minister Hempf. Still, this ultimately leads to disastrous events, including the GDR threat to take away her career if she does not confess where Dreyman hides his red-ink typewriter. After she confesses to Dreyman, her look of betrayal conveys an impossible gaze of death. She has been co-opted, raped, and ruined by the GDR system; Christa-Maria is already dead before being hit by a car and becoming trash on the street.

The film misrepresents feminine *jouissance* in its portrayal of Christa-Maria as an idealized woman. It displays her as a sacrifice like Mary, mother of Jesus, and a scapegoat for the love affair of good men. In *The Lives of Others*, Christa-Maria fails to conform as "woman," an object of desire or "The Woman" that is a figuration of feminine *jouissance*. The film reduces her initially sublime and active agency to an ultimately weak romantic sacrifice.[26] Becoming the dross of Dreyman and Wiesler's archival exchange, she becomes the fallout of the story. Like the "good men" that ultimately retreat from Christa-Maria, the film avoids the real mystery of feminine Otherness. This is a flaw that Žižek echoes when he mentions that women were not usually informants.[27] *The Lives of Others* fails in its portrayal of feminine *jouissance*, leaving no "good" woman alive, and making ethics a male prerogative.

In *Seminar XX*, Lacan links truth and woman, and he calls femininity the "Not-form, a discordance between knowledge and being."[28] As idealized, Christa-Maria makes the other characters anxious but is ultimately killed to relieve the unease. Woman, like art, is the void or mystery that initiates the engagement. Yet the film strangely backs off from this search when it affirms Wiesler and Dreyman as good "men" instead of Christa-Maria and Jerska as the only ethical acts. Jerska and Christa-Maria go beyond societal good to embrace an ethical void at the edge of (totalitarian) representation.

The Lives of Others displays an anxious "fall" (*Niederkommen*) or turning point moment that is an opportunity for artistic engagement. It uses "Sonata of a Good Man" to initiate an unconventional departure from GDR state ideology through Sinthomatic engagement. Not suppressing anxiety, the film is most affecting for its misrepresentative and musical notes. "Sonata for a Good Man" both surpasses and constructs the filmic and historic frames. Audiences bent upon seeing an "accurate" post-GDR film will be disappointed and miss the music that uncannily resonates outside the cinematic reel.

NOTES

1. This chapter began as a presentation by Jessica Datema at the APCS: The Association for Psychoanalysis of Culture and Society 2007 annual conference at Rutgers University as "Surveillance, Subversion, and Seeking in Florian Henckel von Donnersmarck's *The Lives of Others*."

2. Gabriel Yared is a Lebanese-born composer who has been celebrated for his work in French and American cinema. He was born on October 7, 1949, in Beirut, Lebanon, and studied music and law in France. Yared composed the entire score for the film and others, such as *The Talented Mr. Ripley* and *The English Patient*. In *The Lives of Others*, "Die Sonate von Guten Menschen" actually becomes a thematic part of the film.

3. Timothy Garton Ash, "The Stasi on Our Minds," *The New York Review of Books* 54, no. 9 (May 31, 2007), 5, http://www.nybooks.com/articles/2007/05/31/the-stasi-on-our-minds/.

4. Slavoj Žižek, "The Dreams of Others," *In These Times*, May 18, 2007, http://inthesetimes.com/article/3183/the_dreams_of_others, 1.

5. Paul Celan, *Poems of Paul Celan*, trans. Michael Hamburger (New York: Persea Books, 1995), 62.

6. Volkmar Kleinert plays Albert Jerska. According to the "Director's Commentary" by Florian Henckel von Donnersmarck (*The Lives of Others*, 2007), Kleinert was also approached by the Stasi in real life and asked to aid their cause in the theater. He declined but still managed to have a beautiful career, rather the opposite of the fictional character he plays in this film.

7. Ash, "Stasi on Our Minds," 3.

8. Florian Henckel von Donnersmarck, "Directing 'The Lives of Others,'" NPR.org, February 7, 2007, http://www.npr.org/templates/story/story.php?storyId=7238828.

9. Jacques-Alain Miller, "A Reading of the Seminar from an Other to the Other II," trans. Barbara P. Fulks, *Lacanian Ink* 30 (2007): 21.

10. Gérard Wajcman, "Desublimation," *Lacanian Ink* 29 (2007): 93.

11. The sonata reappears in three key scenes. Most importantly, at the end of the film when Wiesler sees a book dedicated to him by Dreyman and written in the same name. It also appears in the love scenes between Dreyman and Christa-Maria that Wiesler watches with interest and when Christa-Maria runs in front of a car to her death.

12. Jacques Lacan, *The Ethics of Psychoanalysis, 1959–1960*, vol. 7, *The Seminar of Jacques Lacan, VII* (New York: W. W. Norton, 1997), 315.

13. Lacan, *Ethics*, 315.

14. Wajcman, "Desublimation," 93.

15. Renata Salecl, *On Anxiety* (London: Routledge, 2006), 34. While we do not know exactly how Jerska commits suicide, he is certainly suffering from PTSD. In "Anxiety in Times of War" Salecl says spies are traumatized by the state in the same way soldiers are. Jerska, like the military soldier, realizes the futility of fidelity to the state and annihilates himself because his "fantasy has collapsed—he thus seems to be literally jumping out of his fantasy."

16. Wajcman, "Desublimation," 106. The political relates to an aesthetic fall since to conceive of sublimation as elevating or uplifting leads to fascism and a false idealism. Wajcman challenges us to conceive of art history as a series of breakdowns since "in the history of art, be it the decline of Paestum, the plunge of Icarus, the fallen Angel, or Adam and Eve chased form Paradise, every fall is finally sublime. . . . Thus the new question: how to make an*other* fall enter into art." At its most open and radical points, aesthetic and politic history requires a desublimating act that entails an imaginative and poetic vision. This work looks into the abyss of the Other to counter the assumption that aesthetic and political structures do not lack.

17. Ash, "The Stasi on Our Minds," 7.

18. Jacques Derrida, *Archive Fever: A Freudian Impression*, trans. Eric Prenowitz (Chicago: University of Chicago Press, 1998), 11.

19. Derrida, *Archive Fever*, 2.

20. Martin Heidegger, "The Origin of the Work of Art," in *Basic Writings: Martin Heidegger*, trans. David Farrell Krell (New York: HarperCollins, 1993), 176.

21. Dreyman's suicide article and the Stasi's repression of these statistics relate to recent U.S. problems. Armen Keteyian, "Suicide Epidemic among Veterans," CBS News, November

13, 2007, http://www.cbsnews.com/news/suicide-epidemic-among-veterans-13-11-2007/, reports that "the US Military is experiencing a 'suicide epidemic' with veterans killing themselves at the rate of 120 a week, according to an investigation by US television network CBS." The film also relates to Émile Durkheim, *On Suicide* (London: Penguin, 2006), as it shows how the person committing it may be less insane than the society or state that has high incidences. Sometimes suicide reflects a societal—more than individual madness—as in the suicides of Socrates and Roman aristocrats.

22. Ash, "The Stasi on Our Minds," 4.

23. Wajcman, "Desublimation," 107.

24. Wajcman, "Desublimation," 109. The object becomes "dross" when it does not function in terms of any material good. As soon as Christa-Maria quits her affair with Minister Hempf, he relegates her to this status and threatens to ruin her career. This secures her abject status in the film. Still, in terms of desublimation, she has potential to be "the sublime dross of art [that] would then be what Lacan said: the highest from what is below."

25. George Steiner, interview by Ronald Sharp, "George Steiner, The Art of Criticism No. 2," *The Paris Review* 137 (1995): 43–102.

26. Russell Grigg, "The Element of Sacrifice in Romantic Love," *Lacanian Ink* 29 (2007): 117. Grigg makes the same mistake of reducing a real display of feminine *jouissance* to sacrifice. He says, "What is so striking about Antigone is that . . . her act remains a true act of sacrifice because it goes beyond the good either of herself or of her city." Yet what Antigone exhibits is neither *eros* nor *agape*, but *philia*, which Grigg's article fails to mention. *Philia* is friendship or family love, and in Antigone's case fidelity to an exiled family or accursed kinship. Also, see Christopher Fynsk, "Antigone's Friendship," in *Infant Figures: The Death of the "Infans" and Other Scenes of Origin* (Stanford: Stanford University Press, 2000), 143. As contrary to the narcissism of Christian sacrifice, Fynsk writes that "it is possible in Antigone's evocation of *philia* (in her words and her acts) [to make] a link with a more modern experience of 'unavowable community.'"

27. Žižek, "The Dreams," 2.

28. Jacques Lacan, *On Feminine Sexuality: the Limits of Love and Knowledge*, trans. Jacques-Alain Miller, *The Seminar of Jacques Lacan, XX* (New York: W. W. Norton, 1999), 120–121.

Chapter Six

Hannah Arendt

Revisioning Dark Times

Margarethe von Trotta's film *Hannah Arendt* focuses on the controversies[1] that resurfaced when Arendt covered the trial of Adolf Eichmann.[2] After experiencing the Holocaust firsthand, Arendt was curious to finally study a Nazi, "*in zie flesh.*" She accepted the job of writing about the Adolf Eichmann trial for *The New Yorker* in 1961.[3] The film is not comprehensive and reduces Arendt's major philosophical works to one tiny chapter. Still, *Hannah Arendt* is worthwhile because it shows the difficulties of representing trauma in history and biography.

Hannah Arendt rarely spoke about her own Holocaust experience in public. As a biopic, the film explores the private realm that Arendt believed was separate from public action and politics. Arendt thought it indulgent or inappropriate to speak of personal suffering. She believed one is much opaquer to oneself than to others. Since storytellers can be less overtly political, they are better biographers than politicians at preserving history. In this sense, the film reexamines history through a biopic account of Hannah Arendt. It draws out the deep personal pains and friendships that the philosopher herself refused to discuss.[4]

In agreeing to make *Hannah Arendt*, the filmmaker engaged in an act of friendship and aimed to show what Arendt could not say. One feminist critic explained how for Arendt the creative work of biography was an act of friendship.[5] The film shows that Otherness of the subject, which Arendt says "appears so clearly and unmistakably to others [but] remains hidden to the people themselves."[6] Arendt was uncomfortable about making her personal life public, inspiring the filmmaker von Trotta to take up the task.

Hannah Arendt is also a depiction of Arendt's deep abiding friendships with women, shown by Mary McCarthy and Lotte Köhler. Lotte was her assistant and eventually became her literary executor. Köhler helps with handling the execution and subsequent criticism of Arendt's Eichmann article. She also reminds her mentor in the film that "God gave us family but thank God we can choose our own friends." This advice proves helpful after harsh critical reactions to Arendt's *New Yorker* piece.

The famous novelist Mary McCarthy had a productive intellectual friendship with Arendt, as recorded in their correspondences.[7] When Arendt's Eichmann article was released, she mightily defended her friend. The film depicts McCarthy and Arendt as an odd couple. McCarthy embodies an "American" literary lewdness that contrasts with Arendt as a dignified European intellectual. Arendt corrects Mary's German and Mary corrects Arendt's English in several funny scenes, including one where Arendt chides McCarthy for her four marriages: "We Germans don't marry all our lovers." Ultimately, these differences were insignificant since Arendt and McCarthy bonded on not always being accepted in the New York intellectual scene; their collaboration and friendship built an uncoming community. McCarthy published *The Group* in 1961, the same year Arendt published *Eichmann in Jerusalem*.[8] These two very different works caused similar levels of fuss in literary and intellectual circles. Both women felt betrayed by unfriendly reviews of publications run by people they previously considered allies.[9]

A friend in the German television industry suggested to Margarethe von Trotta[10] that she make a biopic on Arendt. For ten years, von Trotta refused until she found a *Gegner*, or dramatic antagonist. *Hannah Arendt* is not just a film about a writer and philosopher. Its action centers on the Eichmann trial, which functions as *Gegner*, the dramatic inverse of Arendt's own Holocaust experience. Originally, the director wanted to call the film *The Controversy* but was persuaded otherwise.[11] As it stands, the title *Hannah Arendt* is a misnomer, as it does not fully represent her life or career. All the hesitancies and delays in making the film are part and parcel of the difficulties in representing trauma.

The film is set in New York in the early 1960s, after Arendt's assimilation when she was supposedly situated peacefully on the Upper West Side of Manhattan. Yet, the slightly shabby clutter of her apartment signals the proximity of an unassimilated traumatic past. Stockpiles of paper and books surround her desk, where two key photographs of her mentor, Martin Heidegger, and her husband, Heinrich Blücher, reside. Their juxtaposition indicates that Arendt is not fully settled in. This unsettledness allows her to remember and write about issues of being an exile. The side-by-side photos of Blücher as her current husband—and Heidegger as her former lover—harken back to what Sigmund Freud calls an "Other time and place."[12] These are the remembrances that foreground her writing.

Like Freud, Arendt believed that theoretical works leak pathways that give access to a person's private life. Arendt's refusal of autobiography sounds like Freud when he says, "The public has no claim to learn any more of my personal affairs—my struggles, my disappointments, and my successes. I have in any case been more open and frank in some of my writings (such as *The Interpretation of Dreams* and *The Psychology of Everyday Life*) than people usually are who describe their lives for their contemporaries or for posterity."[13] Arendt stresses the separation and connection of the public and private in a way that's similar to Freud's idea of the conscious and unconscious realms. Both admit the overlap of one realm into the other but explain this overlap differently. Arendt believes the overlap (*of private into public*) occurs through a creative action that produces something politically new, called an event of *natality*.[14]

While Arendt acknowledges that past experience may emerge in her writing, she never actually uses the word "trauma." Her views of violence are contradictory due to the silence regarding trauma in her own life and work. "Crimes against humanity" is the closest she gets to a discussion of her suffering in relation to the Nazi genocide. Arendt did theorize violence and held a tiered view of it as begetting silence or action depending upon its origin. In *On Violence* she links violence with power as a vehicle of silencing.[15] Yet with the Eichmann trial—as with any testimony of trauma—she is engaged in an impossible attempt to represent Nazi violence.

Some of Arendt's work seems to suggest that violence can be sublimated through political or aesthetic engagement. What Arendt calls "action" is a way of working through private trauma by making it into a public discourse. Arendt indicates this happening in her own work in an unusual 1966 retrospective statement on the *Origins of Totalitarianism*:

> With the defeat of Nazi Germany part of the story had come to an end. This seemed the first appropriate moment to try to tell and understand what happened. . . . Still in grief and sorrow, and hence with a tendency to lament, but no longer in speechless outrage and impotent horror. It was, at any rate, the first possible moment to articulate and to elaborate the question with which my generation had been forced to live for the better part of its life: What happened? Why did it happen? How could it have happened?[16]

The film shows Arendt caught up in the impossibility of representing any personal experience of Nazi Germany.

Covering the Eichmann trial allows Arendt to engage in a displaced sublimation. Cathy Caruth describes how in trauma there is a delay between experience and knowing. This delay also occurs in Arendt's philosophy as a gap between action and understanding, such that the latter only follows (*après coup*) from the former. Arendt's view of understanding is like "the traumatic event, it is not experienced as it occurs. It is fully evident only after the fact or as displaced into an Other place, an Other time."[17] Arendt's coverage of the Eichmann trial is an exposure to real historic events that could not be understood as they occurred. Likewise, von Trotta's film imagines the intersection of Arendt and Eichmann as an Other history.

Seyla Benhabib gives a larger overview than the film for interpreting Arendt's own political engagements. She divides Arendt's life into three political phases. The first is from 1926 to 1941. During these years Arendt was a student in Heidelberg and met Kurt Blumenfeld, the German Zionist leader. She was deeply impressed by him and began collaboratively documenting anti-Semitism and the exclusion of Jews from German professional associations. In the 1930s when the Gestapo arrested Arendt, she was forced to leave Germany and escaped with her mother to Paris.

The second phase of Arendt's political life occurred from 1941 to 1960, when she immigrated with her second husband, Heinrich Blücher, to New York in 1941. During the early 1940s, Arendt was also actively working on Jewish issues as a writer in New York. Hannah and Heinrich became renowned intellectuals, covering current events such as Israel and Palestine. During this period, Arendt worked with Martin Buber to conceive of something she referred to as the "Jewish homeland." Their utopian vision was for a federation of Jewish people who would elect councils to guide and govern Jews at the United Nations. When some Zionists believed the "homeland" idea was too utopian, Arendt's disputes with them started to build.

The third political phase started in the 1960s, when Arendt enjoyed what Benhabib calls "citizenship in a new republic."[18] Celebrating the sixties in America, Arendt called the student revolution a "new beginning." Civil rights movements, student protests, and kibbutzim settlements all constituted a moment of "natality" in politics.[19] This is perhaps why she felt strong enough to revisit the subject by covering the Eichmann trial during this period.

It is interesting to note that Arendt also wrote *On Revolution* in the sixties when she wrote *Eichmann in Jerusalem*. With these works, Arendt initiated new discourse on revolution, violence, and genocide. Both texts initiated seismic shifts in cultural discourse, which are still trenchant. The film bookmarks these shifts—and their relation to our own political moment—by juxtaposing Arendt's real life and history.

Arendt's "involvement" in Zionism, particularly during the early period, did not mitigate the criticism during the Eichmann controversy. Von Trotta shows Arendt traveling to Jerusalem for the trial like a survivor returning to the scene of a crime. She stays with her now old friend Kurt Blumenfeld, but it is immediately apparent they aren't getting along. His family teases Arendt about not having children. Still, these gibes are serious and foreshadow forthcoming criticism of her article, "Eichmann in Jerusalem."

Arendt is silent in most of the trial scenes. The court case opens with a rousing speech about the dead of Auschwitz in Yiddish. The speech is heavily dramatic and a kind of re-inauguration moment for Israel. Testimonies are not about Eichmann but history in general. Arendt's analysis of Eichmann "not thinking" offends Israelis who want to characterize him as a Faust, Mephisto, or *der Teufel*—radically evil. Ironically, with *Eichmann in Jerusalem*, Arendt's own view of evil as banal changes from her earlier view of it as radical in *On Totalitarianism*. Her reconsideration of genocide through Eichmann inflames Jewish leaders, including her friend Kurt Blumenfeld, who eventually rejects Arendt on his deathbed.

Criticism of Arendt's Eichmann piece called her insensitive or a "talking head."[20] These critics stressed her identity as a Jew, and perhaps as an arrogant woman, but significantly chose to overlook her identity as a trained philosopher. The uproar following Arendt's report on Eichmann was motivated to a great extent by a sense of racial and ethnic betrayal more than by philosophical disagreement. Her connection to other "white male philosophers" didn't help.

The film depicts Hans Jonas as a ringleader of the critics. He had been Arendt's competitor since attending university with her in Heidelberg. At university, he observed how Arendt was "Heidegger's favorite." Jonas studied with the same professors without the same favor but finally received his Doctor of Philosophy at Marburg. Jonas also immigrated to American and ended up being a colleague of Arendt at the New School. He—like many other European Jewish intellectual refugees—transported the European grievances into America. In truth, the criticism of Arendt as "lacking emotion" is not all wrong. This lack of emotion makes her a strong philosopher but is also a mask that marks her past trauma.

The mask of Arendt's Holocaust experience lets down a bit in the film. In one scene where Arendt is lecturing, a student asks if she was ever in the Nazi camps. Arendt gives a harrowing description of how the French treated her and other German-Jewish refugees at a Nazi detention camp named Gurs, in France. In this place, she said, the women became hopeless and stopped washing themselves.[21] Moreover, one evening Arendt herself lost all hope for herself. She describes how it was raining all day and their straw mats for sleeping were disintegrating. Arendt says she was at this point *Sehr Müde* (so tired), a euphemism for suicide. The film shows Arendt talking about what happened instead of showing actual images of women in the camps. The pain of Arendt's situation is magnified by its recollection as juxtaposed with her current life.

The classroom scene relates to another where she discusses Gurs with her husband. Arendt tells Blücher her survival only came from imagining his rescue. The film shows Arendt recalling herself as a younger woman in France making the decision not to die. It conveys her vulnerability in considering suicide but ultimately deciding not to, unlike Walter Benjamin and so many of her other European colleagues. The film is a reminder that Arendt and many other intellectuals did not just write about genocide, they were also its victims or survivors.

The philosopher explains to the class how she barely escaped with Blücher to America. Another student asks, "Professor, what did you think of America when you first arrived?" Arendt enthusiastically responds that she thought it was "paradise," in an unusual display of her enthusiasm. This scene seems almost disingenuous in its nationalism until one considers the situation of a German-Jewish intellectual refugee escaping from European genocide.

As a New York film, *Hannah Arendt* is a reminder that America, and especially New York City, was once a safe haven and capital for intellectual refugees. The scene portrays America as "paradise" and contrasts with current disillusioned views that have cracked down on immigration and assimilation. It also brings up how supposedly safe Western or Catholic countries (with the pope's permission) gave the Nazis passage. Despite the diminishing of safe passage for refugees and migrants, the movie begins with a reminder of Eichmann's clandestine residence in South America, after he followed a "rat line" from Genoa to Buenos Aires. This connection to *The German Doctor* is a reminder that not all emigrant communities are paradise indeed.

Arendt's *New Yorker* article "Eichmann in Jerusalem" put Holocaust discourse on the map in the United States. Before this piece, what happened to Jews during Nazi Germany was not a matter of general public discourse. Moreover, in writing the article, Arendt suffered from re-traumatizing herself. *Hannah Arendt* is an impossible film about an impossible trial that demonstrates the impossibility of "understanding" or "explaining" the Holocaust. Still, Arendt's philosophical view is that action precedes understanding. Thus, she felt it was her responsibility to act, even if she could not represent all the atrocities of Eichmann or Nazi crimes.

In addition to showing the author's firsthand experience, *Hannah Arendt* displays the philosopher's expert ability to write the *Zeitgeist*. Arendt seizes on Eichmann's description of himself as a "rump roast" being grilled on charges to make a connection between genocide and malaise. Actual footage shows the Nazi sitting in a glass cage like a ghost, bored and unconcerned. In portraying Eichmann as antagonist, the film refuses to pit Arendt against an "evil" Nazi. As the director mentions in an interview, "I never had any thought of putting him up on screen, embodied by an actor, so people could say, 'Wow, what a performance!"[22] Barbara Sukowa plays Arendt as up against an ideology and history, not as another actor. The film's use of documentary footage underscores Arendt's battle with fascist ideology as the real "glass cage" of history.

In covering Eichmann, Arendt does not "explain" a single person. Instead, she considers the whole cultural philosophy that created an Eichmann. Eichmann's unconcern is the opposite of what Heidegger calls ontological care—in German, *Sorge*. This care constitutes the very core of our being in the world as activated. Since he followed orders without concern for or against the Jews, Eichmann is like our modern culture of corporate malaise. Arendt initially diagnoses him as the first of a "rump roast" generation of unconcerned workers who just "follows orders."

Several flashback scenes depict Arendt's relationship with Heidegger and his influential philosophy of *Denken*. She connects Eichmann and his banal type of evil to a lack of thought rooted in unconcern. Arendt's writing begins to flow after flashbacks, not only to Heidegger, but also to the trial. In one scene, she sits on a velvet chaise lounge smoking and recalls the judge asking Eichmann, "Are you an idiot or are you an imbecile?" In Eichmann's responses, Arendt sees no trace of Satanic greatness. He was not even an imbecile. He was simply unable to think. Arendt says it is sheer thoughtlessness, which is not the same as stupidity that leads to great evil.

Instead of viewing the human as simply a thinking substance (res cogitans), Arendt views thinking as a perfomative act, putting stress on the human as embodied (res extensa). It is a way of engaging with, or caring for, the world that is the opposite of just following orders. This view comes from Heidegger's ontology of *denken* and the philosophical question "What does it mean to be as thinking?"[23] *Denken* presupposes the infinitive "to be" as the underlying question. It revises such that thinking isn't reducible to any object or a material body. Rather, it is an activity of being that activates humanity itself. The film shows how Arendt grapples with a politics of care in her own lifetime, even while Heidegger refused. It also gives a glimpse of what it was like for her to have a trusted professor turn into a professing Nazi.

The Heidegger relationship is an unspoken trauma that frames Arendt's life and career. It is another topic about which she refused to speak. Past scenes with Heidegger are imagined in the film as affecting the present. From classroom to bedroom, the couple is portrayed as a bit clichéd. Still, it is difficult to know if this dullness is due to Arendt's time with Heidegger being her more "childish" moments, or if it is a feature of the film itself. The film depicts Heidegger's betrayal of Arendt as a larger betrayal of academia and the very dignity of thought he espoused.[24]

While Arendt incorporates Heidegger's philosophy into her public work, what happened with him privately remains unspoken. Mary McCarthy tries to get Arendt to talk about Heidegger in one scene when she visits Arendt in the country. Their friendship reveals the depth and limits of dialogue itself. At one point while they play pool, McCarthy presses Arendt on Heidegger with a game: "Fill in the blank: Heidegger was the greatest ____ in my life."

Arendt allows the blank to remain as a thing beyond speech. Then she adds: "There are some things that are stronger than human beings."

This answer reveals nothing obvious, but reading between the lines, it suggests that philosophy was Arendt's first love, not Heidegger. The "*thing*" that Arendt speaks about is her love for life that came through her career of writing and teaching philosophy. Philosophy allows Arendt to sublimate her traumatic experience. It helped her survive, love, and work through a life stripped bare by meditation, contemplation, and walks in the woods.

After Arendt's *New Yorker* article is published and the attacks intensify, she escapes to the country. McCarthy pleads with her to respond to the critics, but she refuses to explain herself "to these dimwits." Arendt surely didn't anticipate the degree of criticism received after her *New Yorker* piece. Still, the philosopher became adept at moving in and out of cultural favor. Mary McCarthy's visit encourages Arendt to return to New York and eventually "explain" her Eichmann article, which she does in a lecture to her students at the New School. This cinematic culminating speech is a rousing event that comes at the end of the film. It is not only significant for what Arendt says, but mainly for the act of speaking itself.

Arendt's struggle *with the possibility of speaking at all* is a primary subject of the film. The final speech refuses to make the Eichmann trial simply about Judaism. Instead, it is an opportunity to consider the meaning of the "human" in the twentieth century. In her remarkable end lecture, Arendt reiterates how people who refuse to claim their role in political systems do the greatest evil. Jewish leaders also give insight into the total moral collapse of modern society, not just the Nazis. The Holocaust shows how Nazi camps—and the phenomenon of genocide in general—strip humanity of the human. With Eichmann, Arendt says the modern degradation of humanity does not come through "radical evil." Rather, it comes through a shocking social mediocrity where people follow orders and refuse to think about war, state control, or their overwork. Her final lecture reiterates that the greatest insult of the Holocaust was the idea that Jews were not human. Arendt calls Eichmann's actions "crimes against humanity," not "crimes against Jews," since Jews are first and foremost human.

In a 1943 essay titled "We Refugees," Arendt comes closest to describing her own situation. She describes the Jewish German refugee as generally optimistic, but sometimes she "imagines that at least nightly we think of our dead or we remember the poems we once loved."[25] In this essay and others, Arendt uses the phrase "conscious pariah" to describe a person who chooses to go against the grain and embrace the painful abnormality of their situation.[26] While Arendt does not name herself, the term certainly applies to any Jewish German refugee. Moreover, with the Eichmann trial, Arendt embraces her refugee status more than her identity as an intellectual or comfortably assimilated American. *Eichmann in Jerusalem* did not resolve Arendt's trauma, which was never fully made public. However, it permitted Arendt to sublimate, affirm, and investigate pariahdom in the aftermath of an impossible history itself.

Hannah Arendt shows how the philosopher consciously makes herself into a pariah to initiate a new discourse on the Holocaust. Indeed, as with recent cases of whistleblowers in the United States, these individuals embrace their pariahdom to initiate a once taboo discourse. Moreover, their position is not necessarily to convey a "message" or explain "what happened." It is rather to "change the record of history" and to challenge, interrupt, and resist the paranoiac quest for absolute knowledge. These individuals "act" to reference what has been left out of political discourse. Moreover, they act politically to initiate free speech on unspeakable topics. *Hannah Arendt* makes the decision to witness what has been left out of or eradicated from history. The film is an example of a Sinthomatic invention that foregrounds the conscious pariah who inaugurates uncoming communities.

NOTES

1. This chapter began as a film review by Jessica Datema of *Hannah Arendt* in *The Candidate: Perspectives from an Evolving Psychoanalytic Community* 5 (2013).

2. Margarethe von Trotta, *Hannah Arendt*, 2013.

3. "Eichmann in Jerusalem," Arendt's report on Adolf Eichmann's trial in Jerusalem, first appeared as a five-part series in *The New Yorker* and was later published as a book in 1963: Hannah Arendt, *Eichmann in Jerusalem: A Report on the Banality of Evil* (New York: Penguin, 2006).

4. She distinguishes between the public and private realm in Hannah Arendt, *The Human Condition* (Chicago: University of Chicago Press, 1958), 38, 51, 60–64, 70–73. She emphasizes the different ontological realms as necessary for human flourishing. Thus, Arendt kept her private life and labors mostly veiled, except for the correspondences. Like Aristotle, Arendt believed that the public realm is the world of performative action as distinguished from the realms of labor and of work. Labor, work, and action are dimensions of activity; they are not powers or faculties of the soul, nor are they categories of human essence. Depending upon how we act, we find ourselves residing in the public or private realm. Action is the only human activity that goes on directly between men without the intermediary of things or matter. It corresponds to the human condition of plurality, to the fact that humans live on the earth and inhabit the world.

5. Elizabeth Kamarck Minnich, "Hannah Arendt: Thinking as We Are," in *Between Women: Biographers, Novelists, Critics, Teachers, and Artists Write about Their Work on Women*, by Carol Ascher, Louise A. DeSalvo, and Sara Ruddick (Boston: Beacon Press, 1984), 171–85.

6. Arendt, *The Human Condition*, 179.

7. See Hannah Arendt, Mary McCarthy, and Carol Brightman, *Between Friends: The Correspondence of Hannah Arendt and Mary McCarthy, 1949–1975*, 1st ed. (New York: Harcourt Brace, 1995); Michelle Dean, "The Formidable Friendship of Mary McCarthy and Hannah Arendt," *The New Yorker*, June 4, 2013, https://www.newyorker.com/books/page-turner/the-formidable-friendship-of-mary-mccarthy-and-hannah-arendt.

8. Mary McCarthy, *The Group* (New York: Harcourt, Brace & World, 1991).

9. Dean, "Formidable Friendship of Mary McCarthy and Hannah Arendt." Arendt was not the only one criticized for *Eichmann in Jerusalem*. McCarthy was parodied by Elizabeth Hardwick in the *New York Review of Books*, then later, in that same publication, by Norman Mailer. Arendt and McCarthy sent each other palliative letters. "That the 'boys' have tried to

turn against you seems to me only natural," Arendt wrote, "and I think it has more to do with *The Group* being a best-seller than with any political matters." McCarthy responded, "It occurs to me that a desire to make a sensation has taken precedence in New York over everything else. The literary and intellectual world is turning into a series of Happenings, like the one at the Edinburgh Theatre Conference where a naked girl was introduced into the auditorium."

10. Von Trotta has a long history of involvement and expertise in New German Cinema. She was married to Volker Schlöndorff and acted in the films of Rainer Werner Fassbinder. Her own first film was a collaborative adaptation with Schlöndorff of a Heinrich Böll novel: Volker Schlöndorff and Margarethe von Trotta, *The Lost Honor of Katharina Blum*, 1975. After that, she went on to make many films, including the sister film trilogy of *Sisters, or the Balance of Happiness* (1979), *Three Sisters* (1988), and *Marianne and Juliane* (1981). The actress portraying Arendt, Barbara Sukowa, plays a leading role in many of von Trotta's films, including *Rosa Luxemburg* (1986).

11. Moira Weigel, "Heritage Girl Crush: On 'Hannah Arendt,'" July 16, 2013, http://lareviewofbooks.org/essay/heritage-girl-crush-on-hannah-arendt/.

12. Sigmund Freud, *An Autobiographical Study* (New York: Norton, 1963).

13. Freud, *Autobiographical Study*, 83–84.

14. Arendt, *Human Condition*, 50. The problematic aspect of Arendt's distinction between public and private is the possible suggestion that there is an *a priori* way to distinguish between what belongs to which sphere—for example, poverty and reproductive rights seem very personal but are real political issues. Later works show how the distinction of public and private realms is less a dichotomy that creates norms than a political philosophy that emphasizes art and action in the public realm. Moreover, Arendt believes in the possibility of a move from the "private" to the "public" realm that is transformative or "transfiguring" through performative action. These artists or actors make something new (*natality* appears in the public realm by being performatively engaged—that is, sublimation). Arendt viewed action as the work of creating a reality—the act of making something appear that the private realm does not contain. See also Judith Butler and Joan Wallach Scott, eds., *Feminists Theorize the Political* (New York: Routledge, 1992), 385–403.

15. Hannah Arendt, *On Violence* (New York: Harcourt, Brace, Jovanovich, 1970).

16. Hannah Arendt, *The Origins of Totalitarianism* (New York: Harcourt, Brace & World, 1966), preface to part three.

17. See Cathy Caruth, *Trauma: Explorations in Memory* (Baltimore: Johns Hopkins University Press, 1995), 8. As the Arendt film shows, it is especially upsetting that when a prophetic (radical) voice ends up speaking about (their own or any genocidal Other's) trauma, the speaker may end up reckoning with a double silencing. First there is the structural issue of trauma as a psychic phenomenon that is produced by an unspeakable in language. Second, there is the violent silencing and trauma that results from normative prohibitions in discourse. This is like the criticism Arendt experienced after the Eichmann trial. This type of re-traumatization is common with any visit to a former trauma scene. Although Arendt suffered from both cultural and structural trauma, she certainly didn't speak about her own experience with the Nazis directly. If anything, like Sigmund Freud, Arendt spoke indirectly about her own life through her theoretical works. She might have done this so as not to mix the public and private realm, but it is more likely that she did not speak of it due to the fragmentary, multilayered, and inconsistent disconnects associated with trauma.

18. Roger Berkowitz, Jeffrey Katz, and Thomas Keenan, eds., *Thinking in Dark Times: Hannah Arendt on Ethics and Politics*, 1st ed (New York: Fordham University Press, 2010), 56.

19. Arendt, *On Violence*, 17–19.

20. Some contemporary sources that treat the "talking head" argument, which only exploded after *Eichmann in Jerusalem*, are Dagmar Barnouw, *Visible Spaces: Hannah Arendt and the German-Jewish Experience* (Baltimore: Johns Hopkins University Press, 1990); Seyla Benhabib, *The Reluctant Modernism of Hannah Arendt* (Thousand Oaks: Sage Publications, 1996); Richard J. Bernstein, *Hannah Arendt and the Jewish Question* (Cambridge, MA: MIT Press, 1996); Jennifer Ring, *The Political Consequences of Thinking: Gender and Judaism in the Work of Hannah Arendt* (Albany: State University of New York Press, 1998).

21. Some facts about Arendt's life that are mentioned briefly in the film: In 1940, the French put Arendt into a French detention camp in Gurs for about three weeks. Even before that, she had been exiled from Germany with her first husband in 1933, and she lived as a refugee in Prague until she submitted to the French request that enemy aliens place themselves in camps.

22. Weigel, "Heritage Girl Crush," 3.

23. Martin Heidegger, *What Is Called Thinking?* (New York: Perennial Library, 1968).

24. Likewise, in Aleksandar Hemon, "The Book of My Life," *The New Yorker*, December 25, 2000, 94–97, Professor Nikola Koljević transformed from a literature professor at the University of Sarajevo to a proponent of ethnic cleansing in the Serbian Democratic Party and was, ironically, responsible for "the destruction of hundreds of thousands of books." Hemon wondered how a Shakespearean scholar turned into an advocate for genocide.

25. Hannah Arendt, "The Pariah as Rebel: We Refugees," in *The Jew as Pariah: Jewish Identity and Politics in the Modern Age*, by Ron H. Feldman (New York: Grove Press, distributed by Random House, 1978), 77.

26. Arendt's description of a "conscious pariah" begs the question of the unconscious pariah, or just "pariah." She is careful to distinguish between the conscious chosen pariah and a more determined unconscious situation. Since for Arendt all memory and identity come from the public realm of appearances, the unconscious "pariah" would be part of the private realm and thus without meaning. In order to gain identity, Arendt's view is that the pariah must embrace their situation as an outcast to appear in the public realm as an actor.

Chapter Seven

Gasping for Death

László Nemes's Son of Saul

László Nemes's film *Son of Saul* underlines the triumph of the human in the face of its eradication and despite its utter failure.[1] The protagonist Saul's "solution," his invention, a testament to being human, when confronted with the certitude of being worked to death carting bodies to the flames as one of Auschwitz's *Sonderkommando*, is to bury the body of his invented "son" rather than consign the boy's body to the crematoria with the hundreds of thousands of others. By way of his quest to bury his "son," Saul attempts to invent a death that belongs to someone, someone particular—to a son who belongs to him. He invents belonging precisely in the place that it is being expunged from memory. Saul's is a human aim, a last-ditch effort to say that someone's life meant something to someone, particularly to a father, since by mourning his son, he mourns the future, and the death of his own future. Facing the Nazi eradication of death by the eradication of memory, Saul invents a "delirium," his personal "solution" to the unfathomable horror of the "final solution," one at the origin of human existence: burial and mourning. Saul attempts to find a rabbi, even pulling a man from the line to the gas who claims (falsely) to be a rabbi, so he will say Kaddish for his son. The film tells the nearly silent story of the human path to the name, to community, to history, to the reality of having been, and of remembering. To make a death, a single death, belong is to attest to the symbolic record of having lived. That Saul fails is no matter: most of us fail, but it is the path of this failure whose dignity Nemes's camera is gripped on, not losing hold of it for a moment.

We watch Saul Ausländer, a Hungarian Jew, forced to wake up at all hours of the night, carting corpses from the gas chambers to the crematoria.

He is awakened as the Hungarian Jews, his own people, come in endless droves. At the beginning of the film, engaged in this gruesome and exhausting work, a constant, repetitive, numbing engagement with boundless horror, Saul notices that one boy, while unconscious, is nevertheless breathing, albeit with extreme difficulty. We learn in the film that when any such victims are found to "survive"—freaks as they are for not dying immediately by the gas—they are turned over to the camp doctor for execution and autopsy to "discover their secret." Saul tells the doctor that the gasping, unconscious boy is his son and begs that the autopsy not be performed so that he can say Kaddish and bury him.[2] The rest of the film concerns Saul's mission: he will do everything and anything to find a rabbi and give this boy a burial, something impossible and even criminal in the camps. In the end, Saul escapes as part of the famous *Sonderkommando* rebellion. Here the film uses actual history into which the fictional story is inserted as the filmmakers make use of the diaries of the *Sonderkommando* to invent their story. Saul escapes with a group of rebels into the surrounding woods. During the escape, carrying the boy's body, as he has been for days—hiding it, caring for it—he is forced by friends urging him to run faster to let go of the heavy load in order to escape. Saul relinquishes the wrapped corpse, sending it into the river's gentle current and joining his fellow escapees, hiding temporarily in a wood hut in a neighboring forest. A Polish boy, the approximate age of Saul's "son," comes upon him and his fellow escapees in the cabin. In a silent shot, the camera lingers on the boy's ambiguous gaze and Saul's rejoining smile and raised eyes, suggesting his thought perhaps that life goes on and a boy will survive, like him. Next, we see the boy encounter the Nazi guards in the forest. We hear a barrage of gunshots at the cabin where the prisoners are hiding. These two moments, the boy informing the Nazis of the hideout of the escapees, and their subsequent death, are occluded from our view. Such unforeseen propriety is worth remarking upon in a film in which everything is seen—indeed, where we don't stop seeing, where seeing is blinding. The modesty of the camera in these final scenes is evocative: we take leave of Saul smiling. He does not know what the boy did; only we do. The closing scenes of the film make us wonder about the underside of Saul's love for the body of the dead boy—namely, the speech of the live one that revealed where the men were hiding. The Polish boy's speech is occluded from Saul's sight, as his corpse and those of his fellow escapees are occluded from us.

Saul Ausländer is neither erudite, particularly talented, nor is he religious. He does not even know what the Kaddish prayer is exactly, only that a Jew says it for the dead. We learn early on, although we are not quite sure, that the son he claims as his own is just a nameless Hungarian boy. A fellow prisoner who knows Saul from his village reminds Saul (and us) that he and his wife are childless. Yet Saul, undaunted, insists delusionally on this fiction; the boy *is* his son. Saul's delusion of filiation is the inverse of the Nazi delusion, a paranoid ideology of hatred and disaffiliation that resulted in the machine of extermination. The fact that the dead boy is "adopted" by Saul is not anodyne. By way of this act, Nemes underlines that the symbolic is a fiction; in this sense, all sons are "adopted" by their fathers. It is what fatherhood means, and it is precisely this fiction that was the target of destruction by the Nazi machine, which did not stop at exterminating people and aimed at more than the murder of the person, targeting the erasure of their memory and history. This desire or delusion on Saul's part separates him and his son from everyone around him. It thus not only makes the boy "belong," but makes Saul belong as well. Like Antigone, Saul's insistence on burial is an insistence on life, on a relation of meaning and love. Burying his son, Saul refuses to be a number and insists on a name and a prayer. In so doing, Saul separates this boy from the masses of dead, giving a corpse a death, rendering what has been reduced to flesh once again to the level of a human being. Saul's "giving death" concerns the gap created in the mass of corpses, literally made by carrying the body away and placing it lovingly in the water rather than the fire. Saul kidnaps, or adopts, if you will, the body of this boy; he gives the boy a father, and he gives himself fatherhood.

Burial is an activity particular to early hominid existence. The archaeological record shows that burial of the dead has been with us for 100,000 years; the Neanderthals buried their dead. Homo habilis, Homo naledi, and Homo erectus buried their dead. Burial, it seems, is older than Homo sapiens. Some anthropologists have noted the relation between burial, tool making, and the use of language. It is not just human to bury; it is hominid, a testament to the symbol—that is, to the fact of memory.

In addition to burial, Saul wants Kaddish said by a rabbi, effectively giving the boy not only a father but also a people. While Saul doesn't know the meaning of the prayer, it is nevertheless worth remarking upon here. The mourner's Kaddish is a hymn of praise to God and is composed with excerpts from the books of Daniel, Ezekiel, and Job. The idea is that when suffering loss, even during mourning—an intimate loss—the worshipper is able to praise God. The prayer is an expression of faith, of belief in the face of loss. The "mourner's" Kaddish is actually (in Hebrew) called "The Orphan's Kaddish." To mourn is to become an orphan, to lose a place where you belonged. The prayer reconnects the orphan to God and to a community of believers. The symbolic tie is underlined most emphatically at a time when loss is most prevalent. The word "Kaddish" comes from the Hebrew "Kadosh," meaning "sacred," from the root word that means "to separate." It is a word used throughout the Torah but never defined. "Kadosh" is used to describe God, the Children of Israel, the temple, marriage—in short, to describe what is transcendent, what Rudolph Otto has called "the numinous," or the idea of the holy as "that which is set apart." For William James the sacred designates something radically outside the self. Death, after all, is the greatest separation, an absolute outside.

This "outside" is found in Saul's name as well: Ausländer. "Ausländer" is German for "foreigner." Giving the Hungarian Jew a German surname is evocative. In the language of the monsters, he is named. He is named for what is Other to it. "Ausländer" is another name for Jew. While the word literally means "from another land, or outland," it can also mean "out of this world" or "otherworldly," further underlining the importance of "*kadosh*" or holiness as that which is "not of this world." In addition, the name underlines the position of the Jew as outsider, of his fundamentally diasporic position. Recall that for the first Jew, whose faith concerns a creation that takes place by way of a word, the relation with God begins with an injunction to leave the motherland. Abraham, the first Jew, had to be a foreigner; he had to be made a foreigner to be a Jew. Ausländer connotes this diasporic historic particularity.

The surname also evokes why Saul takes this boy to be his son. Removed from the gas chambers, all but finally dead, still gasping for air, this boy is Saul himself, neither with the living nor yet with the dead. Already murdered by his experience of the camp, by his burning of the bodies, Saul, like the boy, is gasping for death, for something that would tear him from his horrible, gruesome work and allow him to rest in peace. Burial is an act of love and an escape from the Holocaust, keeping death away from its destruction. In giving death to a body, Saul defends memory and thus community in the face of oblivion. Saul's mourner's Kaddish is thus also a prayer said for himself. If not a place on earth, at least he will make a place *in* earth, giving to his name yet another meaning. It is a wish to save his son and himself, his lineage, his dead future, from what he has been forced to do. Everything Saul will do to fulfill this wish will fail—finding the rabbi, saying the prayer, burying his son. We watch as the camera sets in, within inches of his face for the duration of the film, making his failure our own. *No matter that he fails, it is the human choice to fail in this way*. The horror, on the other hand, is what doesn't fail, but incinerates.

Son of Saul is difficult to watch. The camera almost never leaves Saul's expressionless face, coming within breathing distance for most of two hours. We hear the sounds of the gas, the fire, the lifts, carts, and machines. Silence is absent just as death is absent. Despite its enormous success, several critics lambasted the film: "it's intellectually repellent," "willfully obscure," "impossible to watch." "Here we go again," wrote another, "the debate on the camps and representation is officially reopened."[3] All of the negative criticism was summed up by the phrase "Holocaust porn"[4] as the film's new tagline on *IndieWire*. The phrase spread like wildfire.

I would like to consider such criticism from a different angle to ask the question: Why another Holocaust film? Why this particular story, a fiction? Why tell this story in film, and why now?

"Gasping for death" is what we are all doing in what Gilles Lipovetsky calls our "Hypermodern Times." Our lives reduced to working, shopping, and grooming, we are continually reduced to caring for our real bodies over any symbolic pursuit. Gasping for death to have meaning, we are encouraged, even by mental health professionals, to conform to norms, especially in the United States. Or, as Juliet Schor has argued in *The Overspent American*, about the politics of consumption, Americans have sacrificed being for having, and in *The Overworked American: Unexpected Decline of Leisure Time*, she has shown how Americans work ceaselessly for no aim other than the imaginary comforts of goods, and that leisure and rest have been transformed into a new form of regulatory and compulsive work.[5] *Son of Saul* is not only "about" the Holocaust; it is about human beings forced to engage in endless meaningless work where death no longer has meaning. Extermination by work cannot be relegated to the Holocaust, although it may have found its apogee in that monstrous context; it is a phenomenon of our times. The critical difference is that we march to "*Arbeit macht frei*" rather than run away from it.

The Neoliberal Super Ego necessitates constant work because it necessitates constant spending; there is always something else to buy. And by buying, we are part of the machine rather than part of the community. In this sense the film not only tells a Holocaust story but our own story.

The monotonous and horrific culture of the mass production of death and constant work has rendered death meaningless, a condition augmented by the fact that time has been destroyed. The furious pacing of the film and the mechanical noise that accompanies it show the timeless fire of the drive lassoed to the state apparatus churning constant smoke into the stark Polish sky.

Instead of time, we have the perpetual presence of the close camera fixed on Saul's face; the art of film becomes a stand-in for a symbolic loss. Like Nemes's teacher, Bela Tarr, art sustains us as a kind of ethical injunction in the face of absolute loss. Critics have pointed out the debt that Nemes has to Tarr. While Bela Tarr's camera is a witness to a kind of existential void, a sublime and irredeemable suffering, Nemes's camera attests more to hope that that of his teacher. Indeed, we could call Nemes's use of the camera Levinasian; it refuses to abandon the face of the other. We almost never leave Saul's face and are forced into unbearable proximity with him. The film is a stylistic exercise that touches on the ethical imperative toward the other, and like the word "sacred" discussed earlier, forces us into intense intimacy with Saul and utter foreignness at the same time.

The narrative deprivation in the film further is evocative of our contemporary situation. We live with a plethora of information, a cacophony of noise, and a dearth of narrative. Saul's attempt at making a death is an attempt at narrative at its most rudimentary form, a name, and a resistance to the noise.

Nemes captured the noise of the camps, or the noise of hell: the sounds of the elevating and descending platforms upon which the bodies are loaded, the shouts of the Kapos to return to work. It is a noise that interrupts thinking, that makes dreaming impossible, that annuls thought and desire, that disorients, making for a numb attentiveness without aim. Shouts, whistles, a plethora of languages—so much noise in the unforgiving greyness of the camp.

In his book *24/7*, Jonathan Crary describes well the phenomenon of "no time" as a staple of contemporary life. "What is new," he writes, "is the sweeping abandonment of the pretense that time is coupled to any long term undertakings, even to fantasies of 'progress' or development: work is for nothing and no aim."[6] This temporal stasis is marked by an overwhelming sense of monotony. Crary calls this "a static redundancy that disavows its relation to the rhythmic and periodic textures of human life" and says that "it has the appearance of a social world, but it's actually a non-social model of mechanic performance."[7] His description of our world could be applied just as well to the camps: to be a piece of the machine is to be a piece of the state apparatus. The camps are harbingers of neoliberal nonstop production that reduces our bodies to the real and our citizenry to consumerism.

Giorgio Agamben, most notably in *Homo Sacer*, *State of Exception*, and *The Open*, has well depicted this sense of sleepless dead-life, and characterizes it by the camp Muselmann.[8] The "walking dead," the bio-political reduction to bare life, can perhaps be seen most distinctly in today's zombie craze, the "making drive-ridden flesh" of citizens and people. The sleeplessness of the Muselmann should be distinguished from sleep or sleepwalking. Sleep allows rhythm, cyclicality, and narrative. Sleeplessness is the partner of constant work, a popular form of torture, a result of the demand for endless productivity, and it is present in our ever-expanding clinic of "sleep disorders." Ultimately, Crary argues that sleep is an "affront to the voraciousness of contemporary capitalism."[9]

In his passionate commentary on the film, Daniel Bougnoux has written that *Son of Saul*, by way of the title of the film, is a "meditation on all the sons of the future, grandsons, great grandsons, so that they fight against the hate that the film shows,"[10] and he associates the killing in the camps to the terrorism in France. Furthering Bougnoux's point, we point out that there is no article "the" placed before the title of the film. The absence of the article suggests precisely Bougnoux's point; we are all sons of Saul.

Why does Nemes name his protagonist Saul? In the Jewish tradition, Saul was the name of the first king of Israel, whose story is told in Samuel 1. The name Saul means "ask for" or "pray for"; it is made from the root letters that form the word "question"—in Hebrew, *She-ela*. His name commemorates the fact that the Israelites "asked for" a king, even if Saul never asked to be one. Beseeching Samuel repeatedly with their demand, the prophet continually rebuked the Israelites for this wish: Why do you need a king when you have the Lord? Saul's name commemorates the demand itself: Who needs a king for a nation when we have God for a people? And so this young Hebrew, a head taller than the others, was suddenly anointed while he was minding his own business looking for his father's donkeys, his name—Saul—meeting their question.

Saul was "goodly" as well as "a head taller" than everybody else. In the world where representation is anathema to the divine, we note that the king is marked out because of his literal height: something seeable, evident, or—in Lacanian terms, for a trait that concerned his image—something suggestive of the pagan or the idol, what is characteristically *not* Judaic or divine.

Samuel thus rebukes the Israelites: In asking for a King, they did not reject Samuel, he tells them, but God. "Your wickedness is great in asking for a king."[11] Saul's presence as king reveals God's insufficiency. The story of Saul is important because it shows the tension between a religious group that grounds itself in an absolute unquestionable authority and, therefore, timelessness, and a nation among other nations, where futurity has to be negotiated in temporal, linguistic, legal, and political terms. Some evocative parallels can be gleaned from a close reading of the biblical text that allows us to further think of Nemes's Saul Ausländer's "failure" to bury his son as a kind of success that has an unlikely biblical forerunner in the first king of Israel.

In Samuel 1, we read that the first king of Israel, as chief warrior, was charged with executing *every one* of Israel's enemy, the Amalekites. The command to destroy pertained even to women, children, and livestock. After carrying out this command, at the last minute, Saul spared the Amalekite king, Agag, and as a result lost God's support as well as his own authority with the people. Samuel tells Saul that God made a mistake by making him king, and Samuel kills the Amalekite king himself. King Saul made an exception to God's command to destroy everyone. As a result of this "mistake," Samuel would never see Saul again, suggesting that Saul had lost God's approval, and the prophet would go on to anoint David, leaving Saul tormented for the rest of his life. Saul subsequently devolves into a jealous melancholic, mad with envy at being shown up by the younger, more popular, and more morally perfect David.

Did Saul sin? Did he disobey God's command? Interestingly, Saul spared the king, the one who was not a member of the "group" that God commanded him to execute. Saul spared his double, the king, as the exception to the group. Saul is specifically told by Samuel, "Kill alike men and women, infants and sucklings, oxen and sheep, camels and asses." One cannot fail to note that the king is precisely the one who is not alike. Saul does not even know at that moment that he disobeyed; he has to learn it from Samuel. The fact that the two kings have a commonality is even suggested by the poetry of the text. Saul is made king in Gilgal, the same place where he later spares the life of Agag. The word "Gilgal" means "to roll," like a scroll, or the Torah itself. The name of the place itself suggests history that the story sustains.

The story is interesting to revisit when thinking about Nemes's film because it concerns the birth of a nation and foregrounds the idea that a nation, a political nation that interacts with other nations, is "born" concomitantly *with* an antagonist or an arch enemy, an "outsider" that constitutes the group. The Amalekite enemy's paradoxical futurity as "always yet to be destroyed" parallels that of the Israelite nation itself. Saul's failure to execute the king at the last minute guaranteed that the Amalekites would live on, thus guaranteeing the continuation of a nation (Israel) by way of this enemy, making a political, this-world, albeit paranoid reason for futurity instead of a divine one.

The commandment to destroy Amalek is one of the famous divine commandments in the Bible that is never explained, providing the rabbis of the Talmud with much fodder for debate.

> Remember what Amalek did to you on your journey, after you left Egypt—how, undeterred by fear of God, he surprised you on the march, when you were famished and weary, and cut all the stragglers in your rear. Therefore, when the Lord your God grants you safety from all your enemies around you, in the Land that the Lord your God is giving you as a hereditary portion, you shall blot out the memory of Amalek under heaven. Do not forget! [12]

No known rabbis have pointed out the fundamentally paradoxical nature of this commanded and enigmatic "not forgetting" of the command to destroy the enemy. If Amalek were actually destroyed, they would surely be forgotten. The paradox is that the Israelites must "blot out the remembrance of Amalek," and at the same time, "[they] shalt not forget it." One can't help but think of the superego and the death drive: destined to fail, it always succeeds.

In this regard, there is a midrash that reads, "As long as the seed of Amalek exists in the world, neither the Name (of the Lord) nor the Throne are complete. When the seed of Amalek has passed from the world, the Name and Throne will be complete." Thus the failure to destroy totally is precisely what allows for survival, for a future when the evil will finally be wiped out, and for the nation who has always to wipe out this evil. It is important that the Hebrew verb "remember" (*Zachor*) is used in this context.

"Remember" is most often to speak of the Sabbath day; the Israelite must "remember the Sabbath day." The Sabbath is a break in the week, a gap, a day of rest, a day when the original "nothing" of the *tohu vavohu* gets rewritten into the notion of time as a gap in the week. The verb "remember" is also used with regard to Amalek. Even the rabbis have remarked that the two, the Sabbath and the Amalekites, are tied by the verb "remember."

Maimonides himself had hoped to see the end of Amalek. Many later Jewish homilies ally Amalek with Satan, a Christian concept. Contemporary rabbis have opined that "the fact that there is no obligation to blot out Amalek today is only a solution for our modern time but does not provide a comprehensive resolution of the theological question in principle."

While Saul paid for his supposed disobedience with his body and his sanity, he gave way to another body, the body politic, and its sustaining by the body of the enemy. In Saul's "sin" of sparing King Agag, the resulting "loss of God" renders Israel's first leader melancholy; he acts out, debauched and lost. Perhaps we are in a position to understand this melancholia: Saul sacrificed an eternal Other for a human one. In a sense, he did his duty as king; he gave up God to found Israelite history in a nonreligious context, something that is curiously still at issue today. Here we can understand the command to "remember the Sabbath day" and "remember Amalek" together: they are the two moments of instantiation of a negation, one in time itself, a kind of gap in the week, a day of rest, that lets the days start over again, and one regarding Amalek, an imaginary negation to the nation of Israel; both let the other continue to exist.

What is the place of the divine in a nation? What is the place of the nation for a people chosen by God? In his masterful reading of a variety of texts that concern these questions, *The Royal Remains: The People's Two Bodies and the Endgames of Sovereignty* Eric Santner examines Foucault's contribution of investigation and proliferation of new kinds of political power and authority in modernity (the birth of bio-politics) as a crucial contribution to the original Freudian research paradigm concerning the relation between representations and nerves. He is thinking about how a body of flesh becomes a political one. Ernst Kantorowicz's thesis, useful to recall in this context, is that symbolic authority is "backed" by the "sublime flesh" or what he terms the "sacral soma" of the monarch. Post-monarchical societies have the problem of securing the flesh of the new bearer of sovereignty in the "body" of the people.[13]

In his chapter, "Sovereignty and the Vital Sphere," Santner opines that the stakes are high since they concern "the symbolic dimension of the political" as well as the authoritative grip of "how things are done." What's at issue, he says, is "one's own sense of existential legitimacy."[14] Gasping for death, Saul Ausländer gives meaning to having lived. He hears a silent voice, "Father, can't you see we are all burning?" and it is no dream. Both Sauls spare a body in order to make a limit to absolute destruction. Their failures only remind us, as does Nemes's "difficult to watch" film, that we must fail better. Or, in closing, we might recall the second part of the commandment regarding the Sabbath day. "Remember the Sabbath day *and keep it holy*." To keep it holy allows death, the silent signifier of absolute difference, of the "out land," the exception, to encounter a question, Saul, in every breath.

NOTES

1. László Nemes, dir., *Son of Saul*, 2015.
2. The Talmud explicitly forbids the disgracing of a corpse (*Sanhedrin* 47a), based in scripture (Deuteronomy 21: 22–23). Jewish Publication Society, *The Jewish Bible: The Holy Scriptures* (Philadelphia: Jewish Publication Society, 1985).
3. See Maya Caspari, "The Art of Witnessing: Son of Saul," May 4, 2016, https://www.ica.art/bulletin/art-witnessing-son-saul.
4. See Nick James, "Son of Saul—First Look," British Film Institute, December 14, 2015, http://www.bfi.org.uk/news-opinion/sight-sound-magazine/reviews-recommendations/cannes-2015-son-saul.
5. Juliet Schor, *The Overworked American: The Unexpected Decline of Leisure* (New York: Basic Books, 2000); Juliet B. Schor, *The Overspent American: Why We Want What We Don't Need* (New York: HarperPerennial, 2010).
6. Jonathan Crary, *24/7: Terminal Capitalism and the Ends of Sleep* (New York: Verso, 2013), 9.
7. Crary, *24/7*, 9.
8. Giorgio Agamben, *Homo Sacer 1: Sovereign Power and Bare Life* (Stanford, CA: Stanford University Press, 1998); Giorgio Agamben, *State of Exception* (Chicago: University of Chicago Press, 2008); Giorgio Agamben, *The Open: Man and Animal* (Stanford, CA: Stanford University Press, 2012).
9. Crary, *24/7*, 9.
10. Daniel Bougnoux, "*Le Fils de Saul*, Filmer La Shoah?" *La Croix*, November 5, 2015, http://media.blogs.la-croix.com/le-fils-de-saul-filmer-la-shoah/2015/11/05/.
11. Jewish Bible, 1 Samuel 12:17.
12. Jewish Bible, Deuteronomy 25:17–19.
13. Eric L. Santner, *The Royal Remains: The People's Two Bodies and the Endgames of Sovereignty* (Chicago: University of Chicago Press, 2011).
14. Santner, *Royal Remains*, 3.

Chapter Eight

Coppola's *Beguiled*

A History Detox

Sofia Coppola was the second woman in over seventy years to win Best Director at Cannes, an honor she was awarded for her remake of *The Beguiled* (2017).[1] Apparently, Cannes was beguiled. Why remake Don Siegel's 1971 film? What does this new version of the story add to Thomas Cullinan's 1966 Southern Gothic novel? In the precursors to Coppola's rendition, the historical context is at center stage: the Civil War initiating the collapse of Southern Colonial patriarchal rule and occasioning in the ladies, whom said rule "protected," a toxic mushrooming of *jouissance*.

In all the versions, we witness the closed, fearful, and repressed situation of the Southern ladies, enslaved to their own imaginary view of the world and their place in it, as it literally collapses around them. Coppola's more aestheticized rendering of the story, however, expunges historic elements that appear both in the book and in Don Siegel's earlier film version,[2] including glaring Civil War realities, a fiery, strong-willed slave named Mattie, a passionate brother-sister incest imbroglio, and a far more morally ambiguous Union soldier. These historic elements include gothic touches similarly cleansed from Coppola's film: a raven perched on the plantation porch, canopies of dense, sunlight-occluding Spanish moss, and even the brother-sister incest story metaphorized in the "collapsing, dilapidated manor house," all reminiscent of Poe.

While Coppola's ostensible aim is to reveal something about feminine enjoyment as she did in her earlier films, *The Beguiled*, like *Marie Antoinette* (2006),[3] supposes that feminine *jouissance* can be separated from its historic and ideological context. By omitting historic details such as slavery and incest, Coppola's *Beguiled* unwittingly enacts and repeats the very problematic *jouissance* that it intends to critique. Taking the darker and more disturbing elements out, the women in her film appear as a *Confederacy of Dunces*,[4] totally removed from battle, war, history, and reality. Coppola invents her own cinematic version or vision of history, setting her film in the very narcissistic bubble she impugns. In this manner, the limitations of the director are reproduced in the Southern ladies who ignore history and the world outside, perpetuating imaginary wishes and ideals. Similarly, Coppola herself beguiles the audience with an aestheticized, washed-down version of history.[5] Her film is purged of defining historic anchoring points and any ambiguous morality that might be just as irksome to her contemporary audience as they are bothersome to her. Thus, the Virginia plantation has no slaves and no owner, only attractive, well-dressed women taking French lessons and good men who come from foreign countries to join the noble fight against slavery.

Like earlier versions, Coppola's film stages a scene of seduction that rapidly devolves, horrifically transforming nouveau-kitsch-gothic imagery into real castration and death. This is due most clearly in her film to a literalization of metaphor that is imitative more than inventive. It is this that characterizes the film, pushing the story along to its gruesome ending, remarking again upon our own moment in the White-washed (White House) version of the story.[6] This is in part what accounts for another important difference between Coppola's version and the Siegel film and Cullinan novel: the presence of albeit unintended humor. Coppola's *Beguiled* is actually quite funny, even if it aims to be profound. What makes it funny is the reduction of language to an acted-out "reality," as if language could avoid any relation to equivocation. In this sense, her film partakes of her generational, millennial moment where a literalist notion of language trumps culture and history.

In his "Milan Discourse," Lacan contends "to call things by their name is to become stupid."[7] In Coppola's film, there is no play, only heavy-handed symbolism. For example, when McBurney, gardening, says he'd "like to tend their [the ladies] bushes forever," only the authors of this book laughed aloud in the movie theater (and then found that their colleagues who saw the film had awkwardly done the same). Or, again, when waking up to find his leg cut off, an enraged McBurney exclaims ferociously, "You castrated me!" We laughed again. Men did not speak that way in 1864. In the novel and in Siegel's film, McBurney exclaims that the women "*wanted* to castrate him," so they "took off his leg instead," as they would an animal. While he falls down dead at the dinner table from ingesting the poisoned mushrooms, Miss Martha comments serenely about the condition of the roses in the garden and on the state of the girls' sewing skills. It seems like television writing, indulging an utter absence of ambiguity for a lowest-common-denominator audience.

Even Gothic and pulp writers like Stephen King or Thomas Cullinan himself include more complex metaphors and historic references than Coppola. *The Beguiled* detoxes the history out of a ridiculous "Last Supper" scene where the women hold hands and say grace before they feed poisoned mushrooms to their handsome guest. The comedy is a consequence of aiming to be "meaningful," with empty symbols made literal. We note it when a pubescent girl stumbles on a man in a mushroom patch—"What ever did we find here?"; or in the overused motif of sewing that hits the viewer over the head—"Please notice another scene of stitching!"; or in the repeated scenes of women gazing at McBurney—looking through the blinds, the door slats, the bushes; and in their slathering on the whipped cream and sucking it down in front of him. "Wonder whatever that could mean?" A childhood world of language without irony, the experience of her characters is only profound for children who are not yet able to see beyond their immediate worlds. Coppola's "humor" is an unintended effect, a mushroom that pops up accidentally in an overly manicured millennial garden. It alerts us to the way the film foregrounds the ideological confines of late capital neoliberalism: the inability to lack, the fear of the Other and of the other sex, and the reduction of language to sheer mimesis.

Another result of the gluing of language to meaning is a propping up of the imaginary register. Coppola's film is exquisitely beautiful, lingering on long shots of dappled sunlight that threads through the enormous weeping willows like golden needles. It is in stark contrast with the earlier Don Siegel film where the landscape is awash in sepia tones, underlining a sameness that deadens its beauty, indicating that this world was anything but beautiful during slavery and the Civil War. The sepia color, almost brown, allows Siegel to comment on the historical situation, complicating the moral and visual binary of black and white. Coppola's setting, on the other hand, could not be more visually exquisite. As in *Marie Antoinette,* she underlines the proximity of beauty to horror, or as Lacan explains in his *Ethics Seminar*: "Beauty is the last defense against the real."[8] The film shows us that beauty is a defense the women choose as a consequence of the disavowal of historical reality. It is discomforting that Coppola the filmmaker also likes this defense too much, making it her own as what beguiles.

Coppola's beautiful film begs the question: What is the difference between being seduced and beguiled, and is this distinction important? Seduction might connote a possible pleasure. To seduce is to lead astray; astray moves. Perhaps to be beguiled has more of a sense of being transfixed. Genesis 3:13 declares, "The Serpent Beguiled me and I did eat!"[9] "To beguile" means to charm or enchant in a deceptive way or to deceive or trick (someone) into doing something. Coined in the thirteenth century, the word meant to "delude by artifice," and by the Renaissance, in Shakespeare's time, it came also to mean to "entertain with pastimes." The etymological history reveals an increase in secularization from a more Christian ideal to a more fluid early-modern notion of charm. Loosened from its tie to Satan, beguiling nevertheless remains disconcerting as it keeps the tie between fascination and trickery. For the ladies, the distinction between seduction and beguiling is collapsed, and this has less to do with the Old South than it does with new ways of avoiding the other.

We note its repeated use in Shakespeare. Act 1, scene 1 in *Midsummer Night's Dream* declares, "That's why they say love is a child, because in choice he is so oft beguiled";[10] Caesar's power is "beguiled"; Richard is "beguiled" by his reflection in the mirror; Anthony is "beguiled" by Cleopatra; Brabantio laments that Othello has "beguiled" Desdemona and all of Venice; Lady Macbeth tells her husband to "beguile the time" in order to deceive Banquo; and Hotspur is warned he is "beguiled" by the bad behavior of Sir John. One risks being fooled when one is beguiled, and like Eve, making a mistake one partly wants to make. Both Shakespeare and Lacan show that to beguile invokes lack, or what Lacan calls "the phallus insofar as it is lacking," and aims at the lack with imaginary fascination. Here we might remark again on the scopic aspect of the film; there is a lot of looking but very little seeing. While stunningly beautiful eye candy for the audience, it also features women who cannot help peeking at a handsome man locked up and immobilized in their downstairs parlor room. To be beguiled means that we are momentarily stopped in our tracks and lacking. When the ladies realize this, they kill their guest, suppressing any confrontation with the lack that beguiling occasioned.

Freud wondered about beguiling as he listened to his hysterics, and fortunately, he also wondered about his own, inventing the concepts of transference and countertransference. His skepticism allowed him to invent psychoanalysis, abandoning his original seduction theory to theorize infantile sexuality and the unconscious. He changed his mind regarding his earlier views because he realized that the said seduction was fantasy. It was surely not possible that *all* fathers were perverts. Further realizing that the unconscious does not distinguish fact from fiction—that is, it dreams—he discarded the seduction theory in favor of the hypothesis of the unconscious and *Oedipus*, which is the basis of culture and civilization. In the film's representation of the pre–Civil War South, the literalization of the seduction fantasy is the law of the land. There, fantasy and reality were seamlessly entwined. Colonial rule, the framework of Southern "civilized" behavior, was dependent on slavery, rape, and incest. What is interesting in Coppola's film is that she invokes the same literalization of metaphor, not due to the Southern *weltanschauung*—which she mostly omits (and which she mostly ignores or is perhaps simply uninterested in)—but as a symptom of our own contemporary moment.

The use of the verb as a noun, "beguiled" and the ambiguity of the article "the" underline that there is a victim of trickery and deceit involved, and we are not sure who it is. Is Corporal McBurney beguiled by the women who imprison and "take care" of him? Or are the women beguiled, as each experiences an erotic awakening laced with fascination and fear? The introduction of a Union soldier into their Seminary School for Young Ladies underlines each woman's lack, confronting them with Otherness, heteronomy, and sexual difference resulting in the murder enacted to reconstitute the group, a kind of *to-team-ic* sacrifice on the phallic side, to "restore" the "mother's" power and authority, and to suppress any lack.

In the 1970s, Lacan taught that the Real is made by language. The symbolic context therefore is crucial since it frames and determines what cannot be symbolized. By taking away history, Coppola's *Beguiled* risks making confrontation with Otherness a universal rather than a contingent encounter with the Real. This trend to "detox" history, even in art and film, highlights a paranoiac strain increasingly evident in our own time, which involves a narcissistic retreat from sexual difference, an erasure of culture, and a greater fear of the Other. *The Beguiled* reveals the regression in our own historical moment insofar as it pretends to be ahistorical, making claims to universality.

The film begins when the twelve-year-old Amelia, picking mushrooms in the woods, lands Persephone-like upon a wounded Union soldier and brings him back to the ladies' seminary. Yet this Corporal McBurney is no Hades, but rather a much more vulnerable *Homo Sacer* figure, despite the beguilement and maneuvering of all the women. His bloody leg emphasizes the Oedipal theme further underlined by the orphaned Amelia's attempt to rescue this sexualized paternal trophy, like one of her pet animals, from the forest. The resulting toxicity of the mushrooming matriarchy is a postmodern perversion of the Demeter/Persephone myth. In the film, the mother vanquishes all competition to get her daughter(s) back. Recall that in *The Homeric Hymn to Demeter*, Persephone leaves her mother to pick flowers. She plucks the most beautiful Narcissus, which causes the earth to open as she is snatched into the gaping hole by the King of the Underworld, who emerges on his chariot to kidnap her.

The ancient myth shows a negotiation between the paternal and more archaic maternal realms that creates time, literally explaining the cyclical change of the seasons. After a negotiation with Zeus, Demeter agrees that Persephone will spend a season with her husband Hades, which becomes winter due to Demeter, due to Mother Earth's mourning for her daughter, which prohibits seed growth. The myth ends with this negotiation, which creates an equilibrium born of a dynamic relation between the mortal realm—Olympus—and the Underworld, evoking a balance between maternal and paternal power. Such a balance is anything but the outcome of Coppola's film. Corporal McBurney's initial invocation of difference provokes anxiety and jealousy in the ladies, who are overcome and disavow it by eventually killing him, stuffing him in a stitched-up sack and dumping it outside the seminary front gate. Their "solution" to the opened-up hole, the tear in the fabric of the seamless ego, is to sew it up. The ladies' idle embroidery skills are finally put to use. After McBurney dies, it is "as if" the separation between mother and daughter had never occurred, and the matriarchy is restored.

The ladies will remain at the plantation *as if* time and the hole could just be disavowed, summarily dumped outside the gate. Their erotic desire for the soldier is stitched up like the genitals in the Marquis de Sade's narratives, or like a paean to cosmetic surgery that negates the passage of time, as if mortal mothers and daughters would never age. The "as if" is key here, as we recall Helene Deutsch's description of the "as if" patient, an epithet of disavowal and perversion. What hole? What soldier? What mushrooms? We never saw anyone. . . . Killing the soldier and covering up what happened is a Gothic sewing up of history, akin to a Sadean chronicle; it never happened.

When Hades offers Persephone a purple pomegranate full of seeds, it ties her to the Underworld and allows her access to a phallic realm different from that of her mother, and it creates a symbolic place (she becomes queen). Contrarily, in *The Beguiled* there is no fruit; there are only mushrooms, fungi, another vegetative kingdom entirely apart from that of animals and plants, and there is no "return to life," only murder.

In *The Interpretation of Dreams*, Freud employs two principal metaphors to explain the working of the dream: the navel and the mushroom.[11] The navel is the site where the dream touches upon the real. It is so named because it is where the maternal or the real is cut by way of the phallic signifier, the word. The metaphor of the navel implies the cut. The cut is not implied by the metaphor of the mushroom, which just keeps growing—growth being its very means of mobility, hence the popular use of the noun as a verb, "to mushroom." In ecology, mushrooms are known as "cryptic organisms"; they "hide" and can grow "undetected," not needing sunlight to survive. For this reason, Freud refers to the mushroom when he is concerned with "what has to be left obscure" in the dream and what resists further interpretation.[12] Freud posits that there is an uninterpretable aspect of every dream, and he resorts to the mushroom when he appreciates that there is no ending to the way dream thoughts can perdure, woven in the very fabric of the dreamer's existence, even what Lacan might call one's "ex-istence" since dreams concern what cannot be brought to the light of language. Mushrooms grow in dark places (like dreams), feeding off moisture and rising up almost instantaneously where the mycelium is too dense. Freud writes, "The mushroom emerges where the fabric becomes denser and the dream wish arises "like a mushroom out of its mycelium."[13]

The ladies' erotic craving for McBurney arises like a mushroom out of their Southern mausoleum where it burgeons like a mold or contagion out of their psychically dead condition into madness and murder. In a world where metaphor and reality are literally mush-ed, the seminary school becomes an imprisoning maternal mycelium. Much like Ridley Scott's *Alien*, we are reminded that a single mushroom has sixteen billion spores—that is, it harbors a kind of galactic reproductive power. The fact that the 1971 film was directed by Don Siegel, the famed director of *The Invasion of the Body Snatchers*, is germane.

Cullinan's novel *The Beguiled* is more descriptive about the seminary where these women live and from which all the men have fled. First, the word "seminary" in "The Farnsworth Seminary for Young Ladies" is worth remarking upon as a name for a ladies' finishing school. "Seminary" comes from the word "semen," or "seed." Grounded in the phallic, it also recalls the sequestering of divinity students and adherents in monasteries and convents. In current jargon we think of the seminary as a "purity ring" of chaste young people who swear off sex. More archaically, the word recalls the Persephone/Demeter myth discussed earlier. In the myth, Persephone is referred to as a "shoot," and Hades stealthily plants a "seed" of the fruit in her mouth.

The seminary building where they live is a huge Colonial mansion, the late Ol' Master Farnsworth's slave plantation, where slaves and seeds are the primary commodity. Cullinan's revision explains how Martha, his daughter, became "headmistress" after her brother and father absconded with all the money. Without income and with few resources, she decided to sell all the slaves except Mattie, only because Mattie knew about the incest, having also been raped by Martha's brother. In echoes of *Gone with the Wind*, Martha fiercely wanted to keep her grand home, and she "needed the money."[14] She remained on the property, selling her "finishing school" for girls, where they learn the genteel art of pouring tea, a kind of Custer's last stand.

Martha makes the meaning of the word "seminary" literal. She turns it into a space where the ladies remain separated in time and space, protected from the outside world, surrounded by lush weeping willows, locked in by an enormous iron gate. The classic Colonial architecture, the landscaping, columns, verandas, and spiral staircases all remain but are dilapidated due to poor maintenance. The gate as well as the other run-down architectural and landscape details symbolize the women's imprisonment as well as the waning of Southern Colonial rule. Their "education" perpetuates the closed, stifling space of the narcissism reminiscent of a sewed-up womb. The women live sequestered, and the vitiated plantation/seminary becomes even more insular and well guarded. Miss Farnsworth is careful to keep the gates shut and guards against the intrusion of all men, even Confederate soldiers, those men that the women should supposedly be helping.

A toxic matriarchal mother-daughter relationship gooses the plot of *The Beguiled* until the end, when Martha Farnsworth, her arms around her huddled girls, like a mother hen with her clutch of chicks, plans to murder their guest. The girls agree to their Clytemnestra-like headmistress's scheme, despite the fact that (in the novel and the Siegel film) Miss Farnsworth (the matriarch) is revealed to all of them to be false, incestuous, hypocritical, and an outright liar. An unmasking scene in the novel further grants McBurney the masculine role of separating the girls from the mother's suffocating grip. In Coppola's film, however, this dramatic scene of McBurney "unmasking" the mother in front of all the girls is omitted. This is another plot detail the director chooses not to include. Hence Coppola's audience is expected, like Miss Farnsworth's "students," not to question Martha's authority or wonder why it is never challenged.

When Amelia brings Corporal McBurney back to the seminary, every schoolgirl shifts her attention away from her "stitching" to the more engrossing task of seducing the unfamiliar and immobilized soldier, which will turn into yet another sewing project. His masculine presence and wounded body represent an uncanny Otherness that evokes their own powerlessness and immobility. Moreover, as a Union soldier and a foreigner—he is from Ireland—he introduces sexuality *as* the unfamiliar body of the enemy. The women's solution to dealing with this new and very real phenomenon places them in what Lacan would call the phallic position. They turn the Union soldier into the craved-for object, placing him on the side of the woman who inspires desire in all of them. They even admire him while he sleeps, as handsome princes gaze at sleeping princesses in fairy tales. Further, when he awakes, even more in his feminized role, McBurney beguiles and seduces each one of them. After the soldier has already been through the hell of battle, he is "rescued" by the seminary ladies, only to be tortured and incinerated in their feminine inferno. The fact that his name is "McBurney" is no surprise.

The fire that lures the moth is not only found *in* the corporal. The Southern women in *Beguiled* are already beguiled, tricked, lured, and captured by the Colonial and Confederate ideology. This includes the presumption that the seminary should be run like it was when Ol' Master was entitled to all the women and all the property, or all the women *as* property. What we are calling the ladies' "Confederacy of Dunces" is the fact that they imagine that men shouldn't lack; Ol' Master looms unshakably as their masculine paradigm. We learn more about this unassailable position in the novel, where the headmistress's father was accustomed to enjoying absolute privilege. Mattie the slave describes him as aristocratically idle, a result of his absolute license to control and enjoy: "Miss Martha's Daddy was a good and kind man, but he'd rather go hunt quail or fox or read a book or just watch the sun set over the rim of his whisky glass 'stead of payin' any attention to his crops or fences. And his son, Robert, was just like him, or maybe even worse. Master Robert didn't only sit and watch the money flow away, he threw it away as fast as he could on cards and horses and whatever other kinds of sportin' and high liven he could find himself."[15] In this sense, you could say that "beguiling" was part of the Southern way of life that supported a "legitimate" patriarch who owned and ruled the plantation, ensuring its profit for himself, even while squandering it away.

When an injured man in need of help appears, castrated and feminized, the only way the women know how to relate to him (and to their desire for him) is through identification with the Ol' Master. The women, previously occupied by their knitting, French lessons, and cooking, are willing to put all of that away, intrigued by the interruption of the foreigner. His presence breaks their dreamy monotony, invading it with the unfamiliar, challenging their notions of the plantation "family" as an insular and complete economy where all needs are met. Suddenly they are confronted with desires of their own, which cannot all be met by McBurney. Fantasies begin to smolder as they debate how they should handle his injured body and "take care" of him. Hegelian style, they make him into the master, all the while maneuvering to make him into their slave, or secret object of *jouissance*, which in their world means simply owning him. But they are not the real slaves, and as white girls in a finishing school, they can only know so much. In the novel Mattie explains, "Miss Martha and Master Robert were very close."[16] The novel shows how Mattie is the real slave, and as such, she is the one who knows the entire family history.[17] The fact that her role is left out of Coppola's film deprives us of an appreciation for knowledge born from suffering. In other words, the film not only privileges *jouissance* but does away with the way it is seen and known by others who are in a position to suffer from it, and therefore to know something about its mortifying power. In Coppola's film, there is no knowing character for the audience to identify with that would indicate a position of witnessing, difference, or Otherness.

Cullinan's novel uses the shifting perspectives of the ladies' narrations, in the tradition of Faulkner, to complicate the story of Southern land as a space or place not limited to or owned by any one individual. The novel's multiple perspectives make the space of the novel into a rotating narrating and artistic landscape. Coppola's version, on the other hand, makes use of an omniscient perspective, omitting the women's individual voices to amalgamate them in a choral group, a confederacy of women "in love." The filmic version of Miss Edwina (played by the Nordic-looking Kirsten Dunst in Coppola's version) looks nothing like the novel description of her as mulatto. McBurney, after overhearing a conversation and learning the truth of her origins, calls her "Blackie," making use of this information to seduce and bond with her, saying, "Miss Edwina, I think we're much alike. Something tells me we're both really out of place here. Me, for obvious reasons. And you, for reasons that maybe aren't so plain to the naked eye, but all the same I can guess at one or two of them."[18] His guess that she is mulatto is a bond of unbelonging that draws her to McBurney, even though he flirts mercilessly with all the other women.

Unlike the other ladies who feel at home in the seminary "family," and who feel betrayed by McBurney and want revenge, in the novel, Miss Edwina's mixed race make her feel less at home in the seminary and more akin to him. Thus, she bolts the door and takes off her clothes, giving herself to him, despite having been betrayed by him, and is unaware of the plot to kill him. In the novel, unlike the film, her difference from the other women is explained. Moreover, her experience, like Mattie's, marks limits, however small, on the malignant power of the group. At the dinner table, when the girls see that Edwina is about to serve herself the poison mushrooms that McBurney has just ingested, they remark that Edwina "doesn't like mushrooms." Immediately, Edwina understands what the "ladies" have just done. It is an interesting moment, lost in the film, where she resigns herself to having to stay at the plantation, her hopes of leaving dashed. She does not reach over to protect McBurney from his fate but waits silently while he chokes to death. Again, Coppola's version elides the complex perspective, like the fact that Mattie is mulatto and not simply "one of the group."

In Coppola's direction, there is less historical nuance and more reduction. The "patriarchal" problem of the South becomes essentially a matriarchal one. The seminary women indulge the feminine fantasy of a controlling, all-powerful phallus that rules and commands, and that "patriarch" is Miss Farnsworth herself. They fantasize about their absent brothers and father to elevate themselves, which makes them feel more important as well as untouched and untouchable. They identify with a phallic presence that renders them invulnerable, and it is unclear whether it is the absent men or the present mother that does the trick. Instead of relating individually to their guest, where they would risk envy, rejection, and the failure of the social order as they know it, the women prop up the matriarchy to contain the festering of their erotic fantasies, and they follow Ms. Farnsworth, the imaginary phallic mother, who keeps all *eros* in check. The ladies orient themselves toward and circulate around the imaginary father of the horde, the plantation "Daddy," in the form of an all-powerful phallic mother, and the horrific ending is presaged by the very first mushroom.

Lacan remarked on the sadomasochistic consequences of propping up an all-powerful ideal "Woman" in his discussion of anamorphosis, which is a way of proceeding as if the sexual relation existed. He even commented on the place of the medieval woman in a way that could pertain to the Southern ladies we are concerned with here. "She is identified with a social function that leaves no room for her person or her liberty" ergo she becomes the image of narcissistic perfection.[19] Lacan discusses anamorphosis and the "ideals of the lady" in his chapter on anamorphosis in *Seminar XX*, showing what we've been discussing throughout this chapter: perfection as the partner of anamorphotic distortion.[20] The omnipotent ideal can be worshipped in a narcissistic manner insofar as it fixes the mirror, but this elevation or ideal mirror in the sky serves to make the traumatic dimension of sexuality invisible and restores the subject's narcissism.

The fetish serves to suture the tear that the object-as-lack opened in the subject, a kind of "making due" with stitches and hems and seams. Notions of suture and *coupure* relate back to the processes of formation by which they originally occurred. In this sense, we could say that the "castration" or wound of McBurney's leg is the ladies' own castration that so fascinates them precisely because they refuse to see or acknowledge it, preferring a well-stitched seam instead. They eventually suture and stitch back up any desire or lack that is opened by the immigrant as Other, effectively throwing it outside the seminary gates.

In this way, Coppola's version of *The Beguiled* reveals a reversal of traditional sexist roles in all their cruelty. The women are in what we usually think of as the male position, and the wounded Corporal McBurney is in the feminine, vulnerable position. All the ladies take an active role in contributing to McBurney's punishment and death, a reversal of how women were historically burned as witches or put away as insane for arousing men. Indeed, when McBurney says, "I'm grateful to be your prisoner," he's deploying a seductive feminine ambiguous ruse. Is he really grateful? Do we ever know what he really thinks? In the 1971 film version, all the seminary women construct a narrative about McBurney's effect on them; they comment upon how their hens start laying more eggs after his arrival. And in Cullinan's version, he is compared to a crow that struts, takes a shine to bright objects, and flies away, but outside of the effect he induces, he remains an enigmatic figure, like a seductive woman. Ostensibly, the seminary claims to teach manners to young ladies. The gothic irony of course is that they are learning how to become castrating murderers. Coppola's gender-role reversal unwittingly shows that her matriarchy is not feminist but sexist; the murderous women have the same double standards and perversions as the absent patriarchs.

Perhaps this is the history that is alluded to in Coppola's films—not Civil War history or Southern history, but her own. Working through her Italian Godfather and his set of sons, her Momma Hen and her peep of chicks are not so unlike the murderous, vengeful Sicilian mob. Perhaps Don Corleone decaying in the family garden mushroomed into to another sequel. Ms. Martha, after all, in the novel at least, is called the "The Butcher."

Where is or what is the toxin everyone is trying to rid themselves of nowadays? What "cleanse" will work? What does it mean for it to work? And for what? And to rid ourselves—of what?

Totalitarian and authoritarian regimes exploit the absence at the heart of the paternal function, the absence at the origin of human culture, pandering to the anxieties created by this hole, with the aim of occupying and controlling it. Ideology is the way this lack is stitched into meaning so it can be managed and ignored.

Coppola's aestheticized presentation of Confederate ladies cleansed of the Confederacy was released at the same time the debate about Confederate monuments and heritage erupted all over the United States. Can destroying the monuments rid us of the history that we are ashamed of? Are we so sure what the monuments mean? Is saying we decry and abjure the history of slavery equivalent to taking down the monuments? What does saying we decry and abjure slavery *mean*?

It is worth reflecting on the passion of the people who voted for Trump, enthralled to "call a spade a spade," a passion whose murderous terminus Coppola's film illustrates. The expression, now rife in the debate about language and race, is taken from Erasmus's translation/shorthand for Plutarch's original, "to call a fig a fig and trough a trough," which at the time the Prince of Humanists thought less user-friendly than the more popular "spade." The phrase means to call a thing by its name and not "beat around the bush." "To beat around the bush" is an expression that comes from bird hunting. One would hit the bushes so the birds would fly up in the sky so they could be spotted and shot. "Don't beat around the bush" means just get to it and shoot.

In the spirit of this chapter, we might pause on Plutarch's words, at least in their English translation. "Trough" comes from the old Dutch word for "tree," and the fig, well, it was the tree whose leaves were used to cover our original parents' nakedness. Rabbis of note interpreted that the fig tree was the forbidden one and that the leaves of the tree of knowledge of good and evil were used as the first covering, an example of the "knowing" that resulted from this inaugural transgression. Michelangelo agreed and painted the fig as the forbidden fruit on the Sistine ceiling. In the Bible, the fig tree is a popular metaphor for the nation of Israel itself since a fig tree requires cultivation, time, care, and knowledge to grow, just like figurative language. Both the fig and the mushroom concern the breakdown of law, interpretation, and creation as the wake of toxic *jouissance*.

Today, in our present global context, under late capitalism, where we are enjoined to enjoy, we are "enjoyned"; the "lack" is conscripted into the command to consume, a joke played on us that reverses the rule of our biblical origins. It is no wonder that popular culture is rife with the passion to "detoxify." A resulting paranoiac "*discours courant*"[21] propels the entire health industry, and the focus on the body at the expense of the out-of-style ego-ideal is as potent as ever. Further exacerbated by the realities of climate change and the environmental movement, the imaginary basis becomes justified by real circumstances. The passion to detox stems from what is experienced as a toxic enjoyment; the neighbor is all too close. We have to "diss" the "contents" with a colon cleanse. But we are not just contaminated by sexuality in what is now a more and more comforting popular diminishment called "Freudianism." Lacan's point is that the signifier is toxic. Following Hegel, Lacan tells us that it kills. It is no wonder that language and monuments are the new "bad guys." Detox is the answer in a culture where parents don't want to "impose" on their children by giving them "gendered" names or "cars or dolls" to play with. The paradox of the demands of diversity with the explosive culture of hate we are experiencing is apparent in Miss Farnsworth's cosmically ironic comment that "any breath of fresh air from the outside world is welcome to us all."

Coppola's *Beguiled* shows the paradoxical toxicity of the super-egoic command to "detoxify" as the other side of the command to enjoy, a paradox made manifest in the current opiate epidemic plaguing the United States. The Centers for Disease Control predicts that half a million people will die by overdosing on prescription drugs in the next decade.[22] The pharma-con is apparently the American "advance" of the *pharmakhon*. Perhaps history is useful here as well. Where does drug addiction originate in America? At several points in the film the ladies offer the soldier a drink for the pain. Then, when they are cutting off his leg, they anesthetize him with laudanum. Morphine, along with opium and laudanum, was widely used for pain on Civil War soldiers in field hospitals. Morphine, the active ingredient found in opium, is named after Morpheus, the Roman god of dreams. By the end of the war, syringes, sponges, and easier ways of injecting the drugs became readily available. Hence addiction and overdose became more widespread in American society after many Civil War soldiers left the battlefield addicted. America's love affair with opiates continues today, along with updated traumatic uses of Confederate symbols—for example, in the August 2017 Charlottesville pro-Nazi rally. The point is that there is no shepherding of desire but a subjecting of our inner mycelium to big pharma, where it has mushroomed into a national problem of epidemic proportions. The sewing up of desire through addiction and hate speech has become synonymous with enjoyment in late capitalism.

Perhaps if we can finally detoxify, we will become immortal, a wish that Cullinan and great writers before him unmasked as a narcissistic passion symptomatic of a lethal nativism. Immortality, as suggested by the film in the "post-modernizing" of the ancient Greek myth, would of course make the need for sexed reproduction null and void. Detoxification is on the side of beguiling immortality; sexuality is on the side of death and might have something in common then with the signifier that lacks. Living forever, however, would probably not solve the problem of the mushroom; rather, we would become the fungus we are trying to avoid—stuffed, embalmed, and alone, starring in our very own movie, as a veritable plantation of self-preserving botanicals that no one gives a fig about.

NOTES

1. Don Siegel, dir., *The Beguiled*, 1971.
2. Siegel's *The Beguiled* (1971), starring Clint Eastwood and Geraldine Page, is based on Thomas Cullinan, *The Beguiled: A Novel* (New York: Penguin Books, 2017).
3. Sofia Coppola, dir., *Marie Antoinette*, 2006.
4. This is our wordplay on both the Daughters of the Confederacy and John Kennedy Toole's posthumously published novel *A Confederacy of Dunces* (New York: Penguin Books, 2016), which parodies the author's Southern heritage. There are parallels between *The Beguiled* and *Confederacy of Dunces*, including a parody of the main characters and the Old South. However, Toole uses the word "Confederacy" to refer to society, while *The Beguiled* uses the word more for soldiers. We might add that the word "Confederacy" refers to the place the seminary ladies reside and that the word "Dunce" is not gender specific and is applicable to characters in both works.
5. Similarly, the aesthetic preoccupation of the alt-right, their haircuts, clothing, and re-appropriation of Nazi symbols, all show the ways in which imaginary fantasy occludes any historical understanding.
6. Perhaps we might hear something of "The South will rise again" in "Make America great again."
7. Jacques Lacan, "On Psychoanalytic Discourse: The Milan Lecture," trans. Jack Stone, *La Salmandra*, 1978, 6.
8. Jacques Lacan, *The Ethics of Psychoanalysis, 1959–1960*, vol. 7, *The Seminar of Jacques Lacan, VII* (New York: W. W. Norton, 1997), 238.
9. Jewish Publication Society, *The Jewish Bible: The Holy Scriptures* (Philadelphia: Jewish Publication Society, 1985).
10. William Shakespeare, *A Midsummer Night's Dream*, 2006.
11. Sigmund Freud and James Strachey, *The Interpretation of Dreams* (New York: Avon, 1998).
12. Freud, *Dreams*, 564.
13. Freud, *Dreams*, 564.
14. Cullinan, *Beguiled*, 40.
15. Cullinan, *Beguiled*, 37.
16. Cullinan, *Beguiled*, 37.
17. There is another type of "knowledge" in the 1971 version, as connected to the mushroom and as connected to the drives—that is, an affective knowledge. This type of knowledge is associated with the body, and the mushroom as a certain type of mystic truth—Kabbalistic, psychedelic, and of the body. The Kabbalistic is connected to the mushroom, which evokes the oracle at Delphi or the *omphalos* and the buttoning together of the heavens.
18. Cullinan, *Beguiled*, 92.
19. Jacques Lacan, *On Feminine Sexuality: The Limits of Love and Knowledge*, trans. Jacques Alain Miller, vol. 20, *The Seminar of Jacques Lacan, XX* (New York: W. W. Norton, 1999), 220. Perhaps there is something to say about the "Free Melania" movement in this context.
20. Lacan, *On Feminine* Sexuality, 138.
21. Lacan's wordplay is on the discourse that spins like a record that repeats—spinning around over and over again—and the popular lingua franca, or way of speaking in a given historical moment.
22. Assistant Secretary of Public Affairs (ASPA), "What Is the U.S. Opioid Epidemic?" HHS.gov, December 4, 2017, https://www.hhs.gov/opioids/about-the-epidemic/index.html.

Conclusion

Revisioning War Trauma in Cinema: Uncoming Communities proposes a twenty-first-century way forward to the problematic of trauma, inheritance, and representation through artistic invention. The book foregrounds the reconstructed refugee and exile as central to what we call *Revisioning War Trauma* to defend the human in the face and place of its foreclosure or demise. Though the role of art in dealing with trauma has been increasingly recognized, it has been and is being made all the more necessary with the recent resurgence of nationalism and xenophobia.

This is why our conclusion begins at the end, as the consequences of late capital come to the fore in our contrasted reading of Coppola's *The Beguiled.* This film differs from the others in this collection in many ways. First, it is set during the American Civil War while the other films are set either during or in the aftermath of World War II. As such, *The Beguiled* deals with enduring issues of American history, including a nativist view of citizenship that is of immediate concern today. Second, *The Beguiled* does not support, reinvent, or resurrect the refugee—who in this case is Corporal McBurney—but quite the opposite. It kills him; it makes him disappear; it makes it seem that he never happened. The film treats him as we treat the migrants and refugees who arrive at our borders today; we abuse and destroy them. *The Beguiled* is the counterexample to the other films in our collection since it imagines citizenship to be based on sameness rather than the shared difference of the immigrant and refugee who is a cornerstone for reconceiving community. Third, *The Beguiled* is a film that is more imitative than inventive on war trauma in terms of both form and content. In this film, killing the refugee is the result of what seems an inevitable narrative unfurling. Instead of living to tell his tale, the refugee is viewed as an aggressor; he is not hosted or viewed as human. He is reduced to an object, outsider, and scoundrel. The Northerner is imagined to have shown up only in order to steal the ladies' plantation, rape them, and take them for himself to own them. Finally, *The Beguiled* presents a culture of nativism that is ruled by regressive attachment to the mother and makes maternal "law" the rule of horde fascism. All the other films we discuss do the opposite by reinventing ideas of country, and even planet, through traumatized figures who survive via shared ostracism. *Phoenix*, *Woman in Gold*, *The Lives of Others*, *Hannah Arendt*, and *Son of Saul* all feature the immigrant, foreigner, and guest figure as founding an uncoming, uncommon community not based on similarity, universality, or nationhood, but on creative invention and shared separateness.

The Beguiled mirrors and imitates much of our neo-fascist moment. The matriarchal mansion of prissy and privileged Southern women dressed in plantation white resembles those Neo-Nazis, Confederates, and purists who want to "make America great again." All guests, foreigners, immigrants, and anyone from the outside that is not considered "native" are perceived as a threat. Lacan explains how anxiety regarding the "non-native" is simply an imaginary wish for wholeness in the maternal. He explains in *Seminar X* that "anxiety is when there appears in this frame something which is already there much closer to home: *Heim*, the guest (*l'hote*) you will say, and in a certain sense, of course this unknown guest who appears in an unexpected fashion has a good deal to do with what is met with in the *Unheimlich*."[1] The guest, an object of anxiety, brings up a deeper truth, which is that *desire is always desire of the Other*. Another way of saying this is that we exist as castrated in the original foreignness of language, which is our first home but one which never completely allows us to feel at home.

The uncanny guest elicits anxiety as a reminder that our home in language begins with the cut in signification and an opening to the real. We are all guests, and thus neighbors of a shared language, which is also a reminder that we are all transient. A regressive wish to kill the guest pervades *The Beguiled*. This hostile reaction to the guest is actually less uncanny than the reactions in the other films of our collection since it does not engage the guest as an impetus for reinvention. Rather, *The Beguiled* is more on the side of gothic horror—that is, the anxiety is silly. *The Beguiled* presents a mimetic community that is not uncoming, but believes itself to have already arrived as the incarnation of the original American South. The paranoid women who rule the nest are hostile toward all guests by foreclosing lack and Otherness, making their mansion a suffocating, incestuous, matriarchal prison.

All the films in *Revisioning War Trauma in Cinema: Uncoming Communities* deal with issues of guest-host hostility or hospitality and uncanniness as it concerns the foreignness of our originary thrownness into language. The way characters consider "home" concerns their relation to language and culture, as well as their relation to the "Other." The extent to which a guest is welcome or unwelcome indicates the civility or incivility of that particular society. It also indicates the way a culture deals with war and its aftermath, including legacy, inheritance, and citizenship. Most of the traumatized figures in our films are not welcome in their homeland and re-create themselves in foreign lands. Hospitality is indicative of how well aligned an existential state or public realm is with originary foreignness; it is not just a contemporary American problem in the age of Trump. It concerns the origins of civilization and language as the unhomely home of being itself. Generally, foreigners and even citizens who have never left home feel most familiar in their mother tongue.

The inventiveness of foreigners is their connection to *lalague*, which is another way of saying "the mother tongue." What Jacques Lacan calls "*lalangue*" is the closest one gets to carving out a real home in language and is thus often the impetus for Sinthomatic invention. It "is something that remains indeterminate (*indécis*) between the phoneme, the word, the sentence, and even the whole of thought."[2] *Lalangue* is our homeland. We speak in the place we feel most homely. As Derrida mentions, "The exiles, the deported, the expelled, the stateless, rootless, lawless nomads absolute foreigners often continue to recognize the language that is called the mother tongue as their ultimate homeland and even their last resting place. That was Hannah Arendt's response on one occasion: she no longer felt German except in language, as though the language were a remains of belonging, although in fact . . . , language is also the experience of expiration of an irreducible expropriation."[3] The point is that the foreigner is not any more related to a mother tongue than anyone else. Rather, the foreigner reminds us of the fact that language is an originary Other in which no one is ever fully at home. *Lalangue* is like the mother tongue, as already "the other's language," which the foreigner brings into play. Even though the "mother tongue" is a shared language and thus is never entirely representative, many of the figures in our films use it for invention. Their mother tongue is host and offers *Xenia* through the *patois*, which houses the foreigner even in exile. It is a homeland and a resting place for war-traumatized figures in situations of absolute hostility.

This kind of Joycean invention through *lalangue* is antithetical to a language that fixes meaning marrying it to power. Such a fixation tries to imaginarily negate the real, the void with which all language has to deal. We see this when the "ladies" in *The Beguiled* foreclose the guest, cutting off his leg and ultimately poisoning him to avoid an anxiety that would question their being and power. The linchpin in this kind of imaginary stasis is the woman as phallic. The other films in this book reveal a different relation to woman as the basis of the Sinthome; as Jacques Lacan explains, "A woman is a sinthome for every man."[4] In the other films, there is a connection between significance and feminine *jouissance*, precisely what limits language and shows its incompleteness. Instead of writing the real, *Revisioning War Trauma* revisions a filmic reel that welcomes feminine *jouissance*.

The Greek term *xenia*, which means "hospitality," was a ruling principle in ancient societies. Hospitality was considered an ethical indicator of whether a region or person was civilized and safe or brutish and base. Indeed, while a ruler like King Sisyphus of Corinth temporarily got away with killing travelers and guests to maintain his iron grip, his violation of *xenia* and bad treatment of guests was eventually punished. This is akin to the wish to expel the Other, the guest, the indicator of lack, difference, and the outside world. In the underworld, Sisyphus was reduced to a futile existence and condemned to endlessly roll a huge boulder up a steep hill. Sisyphus held the hubristic belief that his cleverness surpassed Zeus's. Likewise, refugees in the films prefigure our contemporary moment where nativist pride refuses asylum for guests.

Ancient canonical texts are clear about hospitality as a necessary social value. The consequences of hostility toward guests are shown in *The Odyssey* with the cyclops Polyphemus, who is punished not only for imprisoning Odysseus and crew, but for eating them. When Odysseus blinds his one eye, castrating the monster so that he is no longer able to spot an Other to eat, Polyphemus famously yells that "Nobody" is the name of the one who blinded him. This nobody is his eternal inability to name anyone, even the one who punished him. The cyclops is the Ur bad host, and *The Odyssey* describes him as a "grim-loner, dead set in his own lawless ways. . . . Built like no mortal who ever supped on bread, no. . . . like a shaggy peak, I'd say a man mountain rearing head and shoulders over the world."[5] Many of the films in this book, like *Phoenix*, feature monstrous family members, as in Nelly's case, where her husband not only betrays her but sends her to be consumed by the fires of the death camps. The films in our collection show how authoritarian states contain citizens who respond to anxiety by foreclosing all Otherness and even their very human need for society. Polyphemus felt no need for guests because they threatened his place in the maternal cave. Today, American refugees and immigrants are caught at the border like the visitors to the cyclops; they are the raw meat that Trump feeds his hungry base, who similarly guard their own "private" property.

This book holds the premise that the rise of authoritarian nationalism is the result of anxiety regarding the Other. Since we do not always learn from history, and often have a penchant for irrationally repeating the same mistakes, *Revisioning War Trauma in Cinema: Uncoming Communities* makes use of that anxiety for artistic engagement. The book explores films that are testimony and that allow the viewer to feel the dwindling of autonomy that accompanies authoritarianism and mass obedience. It responds to curiosities about the supposedly bygone world of enlightenment authoritarianism and considers how to stop its reoccurrence. The films expose postwar trauma and follow survivors of an authoritarian regime, who, like Victor Klemperer, documented enduring daily life under Nazism. These films allow the viewer to see, hear, and feel societies unravel from one of their survivors. Like Klemperer's diaries, the films document the everyday progression of tyranny as both a witness and a cautionary.

Klemperer's diaries do not attempt to represent history but allow the reader to feel the effects of rising nationalism on his own street. He records a summary of Hitler's election speech: "I know of no intellectuals, bourgeois, proletarians, only the people. Why have millions of my opponents remained in the country? The émigrés are 'scoundrels' like the Rasser brothers. And a couple of hundred thousand rootless internationalists—interruption: 'Jews!'—want to set nations of millions at one another's throats . . . *I* only want peace. I have risen from the common people. I want nothing for myself."[6] The diaries repeat Hitler's words, which pivot around the phrase "my people" and "the common people," as if the state could determine who is related. This language is meant to control who belongs by regulating the state, *heimat*, and all citizens as family. This rhetoric that demonizes the "rootless émigrés" as scoundrels is typical of our national discourse today. Klemperer's diaries, like our collection, provide a different perspective on the rise of an authoritarian and xenophobic regime. Since hospitable "survival" is rarely accomplished through rational argumentation, *Revisioning War Trauma in Cinema* facilitates revisioning via shock, or a shout out to the viewer to "Wake up!" It draws attention to films that reel around the unconscious effects of repetition compulsion in history.

This book, like Klemperer's diaries, does not explain history but hosts and welcomes films that show the effects of postwar trauma and rising nationalism on everyday citizens. Tyranny involves an interruption of the everyday realm in society, and human privacy itself, such that the state becomes the monstrous "host." As Derrida mentions in this regard, "From the moment when a public authority, a State, this or that State power, gives itself or is recognized as having the right to control, monitor, ban exchanges that those doing the exchanging deem private, but that the State can intercept since these private exchanges cross public space and become available there, then every element of hospitality gets disrupted."[7] Inhospitality amounts to existential situations that transgress the line between public and private. Instead of *sorge*, or care, these transgressions capitalize off the border of our originary foreignness as both familiar and unfamiliar.

Revisioning War Trauma in Cinema: Uncoming Communities goes beyond history to witness the affective and irrational event of democracy breaking down. A century after films like Fritz Lang's *The Testament of Dr. Mabuse* (1933),[8] we are concerned with a reel that does not show the world sliding toward fascism but its aftermath. Unlike history, which eschews the unofficial, art lets us see worlds of testimony beside the officially reported information. Victor Klemperer's diaries remained unpublished for thirty-five years after his death. Then, in 1995, the German publishing house Aufbau Verlag finally printed two volumes covering the years from 1933 to 1945. Random House issued an English translation only in 1998 and 1999, and did not bring the third volume into print in the United States.[9] These diaries, like the films in our collection, are finding new readers today for their relevance on enduring quotidian life under fascism.

Authoritarian regimes are not overturned through reason but by an affective turn that is a renewed zeitgeist. Instead of working through plot or storyline, these films work through Sinthomatic experience: the lapsus, the interruption, the impediment. Touching on the real, many of them make the viewer feel lost: What am I supposed to think? How am I supposed to understand? As a result, viewers leave the theater more careful and taciturn, left with the impossible *jouissance* and loss that undergirds the film. *Revisioning War Trauma in Cinema: Uncoming Communities* works around what Jacques Lacan calls "the Sinthome which is situated at the place where the knot slips, where there is a lapsus of the knot. A knot is something which fails. Likewise, it is due to the consistency of the unconscious that there are heaps of failures."[10] Instead of sending a message or presenting or buttressing a given ideology, the films convey a knot—that is, the hole of trauma. Figures in these films negotiate traumatic not whole situation of exile and loss affectively. If there is sense to be made from *Revisioning War Trauma*, it is that xenophobic nationalism does not make sense. The aesthetic aspect of the Sinthome redirects anxiety to engage the body and the cinematic reel in a way that undercuts the imaginary seamlessness of authoritarian belonging.

Revisioning War Trauma in Cinema: Uncoming Communities features films that engage in an aesthetic practice of circling around the hole, which is trauma, in order to invent. This type of invention is the antidote to nativism and nation building, which foreclose the anxiety occasioned by the foreigner and guest. Our contemporary moment of global peril is one where anyone and everyone is potentially an unwelcome guest, a refugee. The refugee or exile is a paradigmatic figure for negotiating anxiety, a barometer of national civility, construction, and invention. Our filmic *Homo Sacer* is a figure "for the people," who drives a hosting of the guest, which allows citizens to become people once again. This book focuses on the war traumatized, refugees, and exiles because they serve as a historical mirror that reflects our own impasses—namely, and most dramatically, the Western neoliberal crisis of identity. These films embrace the survivor as a paradigmatic figure for negotiating post-nationhood and a global situation that threatens to make us all strangers and foreigners on our fragile planet.

NOTES

1. Jacques Lacan, Bruce Fink, and Jacques Lacan, *On Feminine Sexuality: The Limits of Love and Knowledge; Encore 1972–1973*, vol. X, The Seminar of Jaques Lacan, Jacques Lacan. Transl. with notes by Bruce Fink; Book 20 (New York: Norton, 1999), 65.
2. Lacan, *On Feminine Sexuality*, 143.
3. Jacques Derrida, *Of Hospitality: Cultural Memory in the Present*, trans. Anne Dufourmantelle (Stanford, CA: Stanford University Press, 2000), 89.
4. Jacques Lacan, *The Sinthome: The Seminar of Jacques Lacan, Book XXIII*, 1st ed. (Cambridge, UK: Polity, 2016), 44.
5. Homer, *The Odyssey*, trans. Robert Fagles (New York: Penguin, 1997), 217.
6. Victor Klemperer, *I Shall Bear Witness: The Diaries of Victor Klemperer 1933–41* (London: Phoenix, 2003), 49–50.
7. Derrida, *Of Hospitality*, 51.
8. Fritz Lang, dir., *The Testament of Dr. Mabuse*, 1933.
9. Victor Klemperer and Martin Chalmers, *I Will Bear Witness: A Diary of the Nazi Years, 1942–1945* (New York: Modern Library, 2001); Victor Klemperer and Martin Chalmers, *The Lesser Evil: The Diaries of Victor Klemperer 1945–1959* (London: Phoenix, 2004).
10. Lacan, *Sinthome*, 43.

Bibliography

Assistant Secretary of Public Affairs. "What Is the U.S. Opioid Epidemic?" HHS.gov, December 4, 2017.

Agamben, Giorgio. *Homo Sacer 1: Sovereign Power and Bare Life*. Stanford, CA: Stanford University Press, 1998.

———. *The Open: Man and Animal*. Stanford, CA: Stanford University Press, 2012.

———. *State of Exception*. Homo sacer. Chicago: University of Chicago Press, 2008.

Anonymous. *A Woman in Berlin: Eight Weeks in the Conquered City : A Diary*. Translated by Philip Boehm and Marta Hillers. New York: Picador/Henry Holt, 2006.

Arendt, Hannah. *Eichmann in Jerusalem: A Report on the Banality of Evil*. New York: Penguin, 2006.

———. *The Human Condition*. Chicago: University of Chicago Press, 1958.

———. *Men in Dark Times*. New York: Harcourt, Brace & World, 1968.

———. *On Violence*. New York: Harcourt, Brace, Jovanovich, 1970.

———. *The Origins of Totalitarianism*. New York: Harcourt, Brace & World, 1966.

———. "The Pariah as Rebel: We Refugees." In *The Jew as Pariah: Jewish Identity and Politics in the Modern Age*, edited by Ron H. Feldman, 55–67. New York: Grove Press, distributed by Random House, 1978.

———. "We Refugees." *Menorah Journal* 31, no. 1 (1943): 69–77.

Arendt, Hannah, Mary McCarthy, and Carol Brightman. *Between Friends: The Correspondence of Hannah Arendt and Mary McCarthy, 1949–1975*. 1st ed. New York: Harcourt Brace, 1995.

Ash, Lucy. "The Rape of Berlin." *BBC News*, May 1, 2015.

Ash, Timothy Garton. "The Stasi on Our Minds." *The New York Review of Books* 54, no. 9 (May 31, 2007).

Auden, Wystan Hugh. "The Unknown Citizen." In *Selected Poems*, 93. New York: Vintage International, 2007.

Auster, Paul, Maurice Blanchot, Lydia Davis, Robert Lamberton, and George Quasha. *The Station Hill Blanchot Reader: Fiction & Literary Essays*. Barrytown, NY: Station Hill/Barrytown, Ltd, 1999.

Bachelard, Gaston. *The Psychoanalysis of Fire*. Edited by Northrop Frye, 2015.

Barnouw, Dagmar. *Visible Spaces: Hannah Arendt and the German-Jewish Experience*. Baltimore: Johns Hopkins University Press, 1990.

Benhabib, Seyla. "Hannah Arendt's Political Engagements." In *Thinking in Dark Times: Hannah Arendt on Ethics and Politics*, edited by Roger Berkowitz, Jeffrey Katz, and Thomas Keenan, 55–61. New York: Fordham University Press, 2010.

———. *The Reluctant Modernism of Hannah Arendt*. Thousand Oaks: Sage Publications, 1996.
Benjamin, Walter. "Theses on the Philosophy of History." In *Illuminations*, edited by Hannah Arendt, translated by Harry Zohn, 253–64. New York: Harcourt, Brace & World, 1968.
Berkowitz, Roger, Jeffrey Katz, and Thomas Keenan, eds. *Thinking in Dark Times: Hannah Arendt on Ethics and Politics*. New York: Fordham University Press, 2010.
Bernstein, Richard J. *Hannah Arendt and the Jewish Question*. Cambridge, MA: MIT Press, 1996.
Bettelheim, Bruno. *The Uses of Enchantment: The Meaning and Importance of Fairy Tales*. New York: Random House Inc., 2010.
Blanchot, Maurice. *The Unavowable Community*. Barrytown, NY: Station Hill, 1988.
———. *The Writing of the Disaster*. Translated by Ann Smock. Lincoln: University of Nebraska Press, 1995.
Bougnoux, Daniel. "*Le Fils de Saul*, Filmer La Shoah?" *La Croix*, November 5, 2015.
Buber, Martin. *I and Thou*. Translated by Walter Kaufmann. Edinburgh: T & T Clark, 1975.
Butler, Judith, and Joan Wallach Scott, eds. *Feminists Theorize the Political*. New York: Routledge, 1992.
Caruth, Cathy. *Literature in the Ashes of History*. Baltimore: Johns Hopkins University Press, 2013.
———. "Lying and History." In *Thinking in Dark Times: Hannah Arendt on Ethics and Politics*, edited by Roger Berkowitz, Jeffrey Katz, and Thomas Keenan, 79–92. New York: Fordham University Press, 2010.
———. *Trauma: Explorations in Memory*. Baltimore: Johns Hopkins University Press, 1995.
———. *Unclaimed Experience: Trauma, Narrative, and History*. Baltimore: Johns Hopkins University Press, 1996.
Caspari, Maya. "The Art of Witnessing: Son of Saul," *ICA* Bulletin, May 4, 2016. https://www.ica.art/bulletin/art-witnessing-son-saul.
Celan, Paul. *Poems of Paul Celan*. Translated by Michael Hamburger. New York: Persea Books, 1995.
Chiesa, Lorenzo. *Subjectivity and Otherness: A Philosophical Reading of Lacan*. Cambridge, MA: MIT Press, 2007.
Clooney, George, dir. *The Monuments Men*. 2014.
Cohen, A. *The Babylonian Talmud: Tractate Berākōt: Translated into English for the First Time, with Introduction, Commentary, Glossary and Indices*. Cambridge: Cambridge University Press, 2013.
Coppola, Sofia, dir. *The Beguiled*. 2017.
———. *Marie Antoinette*. 2006.
Crary, Jonathan. *24/7: Terminal Capitalism and the Ends of Sleep*. New York: Verso, 2013.
Cullinan, Thomas. *The Beguiled: A Novel*. New York: Penguin Books, 2017.
Curtis, Simon, dir. *Woman in Gold*. 2015.
Dean, Michelle. "The Formidable Friendship of Mary McCarthy and Hannah Arendt." *The New Yorker*, June 4, 2013.
Deleuze, Gilles. *Masochism: Coldness and Cruelty*. New York: Zone Books, 1991.
Derrida, Jacques. *Archive Fever: A Freudian Impression*. Translated by Eric Prenowitz. Chicago: University of Chicago Press, 1998.
———. *Of Hospitality*. Translated by Anne Dufourmantelle. Cultural Memory in the Present. Stanford, CA: Stanford University Press, 2000.
Deutsch, Helene. *Psychology of Women: A Psychoanalytic Interpretation*. New York: Grune & Stratton, 1980.
Donnersmarck, Florian Henckel von. "Directing 'The Lives of Others.'" NPR.org, February 7, 2007. http://www.npr.org/templates/story/story.php?storyId=7238828.
———, dir. *The Lives of Others*. 2007.
Durkheim, Émile. *On Suicide*. London: Penguin, 2006.
Fagles, Robert. *Sophocle—The Three Theban Plays: Antigone, Oedipus the King, Oedipus at Colonus*. New York: Penguin, 2004.

Fahrenthold, David. "Trump Recorded Having Extremely Lewd Conversation about Women in 2005." *Washington Post*, October 8, 2016.
Fallada, Hans. *Alone in Berlin.* Translated by Michael Hofmann. London: Penguin Classics, 2009.
Färberböck, Max, dir. *The Downfall of Berlin: Anonyma*. Strand, 2008.
Freud, Sigmund. *An Autobiographical Study*. New York: Norton, 1963.
———. "Constructions in Analysis." In *The Standard Edition of the Complete Psychological Works of Sigmund Freud*, translated by James Strachey, 255–70. London: Hogarth Press, 1964.
———. "The Economic Problem of Masochism." In *Collected Papers*, edited by James Strachey, vol. 5, 255–68. London: The Hogarth Press, 1950.
———. *Group Psychology and the Analysis of the Ego*. Translated by Ethel Spector Person. Hillsdale, NJ: Analytic Press, 2001.
———. "The Taboo of Virginity." In *Standard Edition of the Complete Psychological Works of Sigmund Freud*, vol. 11, 193–218. London: Hogarth Press, 1957.
Freud, Sigmund, and James Strachey. *The Interpretation of Dreams*. New York: Avon, 1998.
Fynsk, Christopher. "Antigone's Friendship." In *Infant Figures: The Death of the "Infans" and Other Scenes of Origin*, 131–46. Stanford, CA: Stanford University Press, 2000.
Grigg, Russell. "The Element of Sacrifice in Romantic Love." *Lacanian Ink* 29 (2007): 114–20.
Grossman, Atina. "A Question of Silence: The Rape of German Women by Occupation Soldiers." *October* 72 (1995): 43–63.
Han, Byung-Chul, Alain Badiou, and Erik Butler. *The Agony of Eros*. Cambridge, MA: MIT Press, 2017.
Heidegger, Martin. "The Origin of the Work of Art." In *Basic Writings: Martin Heindegger*, translated by David Farrell Krell, 143–88. New York: HarperCollins, 1993.
———. *Poetry, Language, Thought.* New York: Harper & Row, 1971.
———. *What Is Called Thinking?* New York: Perennial Library, 1968.
Hemon, Aleksandar. "The Book of My Life." *The New Yorker*, December 25, 2000.
Hitchcock, Alfred. *Vertigo*. 1958.
Hoffmann, E. T. A, Leonard J Kent, and Elizabeth C Knight. *Tales of E.T.A. Hoffmann.* Chicago: University of Chicago Press, 1974.
Homer. *The Odyssey*. Translated by Robert Fagles. London: Penguin, 1997.
"Interview with Mossad Agent: 'We Could Have Killed Mengele.'" *Spiegel Online*, September 8, 2008.
"Israeli Woman Killed by Nazis in Argentina; Sought Nazi War Criminal." *Jewish Telegraphic Agency*, March 22, 1961.
James, Nick. "Son of Saul—First Look." British Film Institute, December 14, 2015.
James, William. *The Varieties of Religious Experience: A Study in Human Nature*. New York: The Modern Library (Parkway Printing Co.), 1902.
Jewish Publication Society. *The Jewish Bible: The Holy Scriptures*. Philadelphia, PA: Jewish Publication Society, 1985.
"Just Following Orders: Erich Priebke." *The Economist*, October 26, 2013.
Kantorowicz, Ernst Hartwig, and Conrad Leyser. *The King's Two Bodies: A Study in Mediaeval Political Theology*. Princeton N.J.: Princeton University Press, 2016.
Kasher, Hannah. "Parashat Ki Tetze 5760/2000." Bar-Ilan University's Parashat Hashavua Study Center, September 9, 2000.
Keteyian, Armen. "Suicide Epidemic Among Veterans." CBS News, November 13, 2007.
Klemperer, Victor. *I Shall Bear Witness: The Diaries of Victor Klemperer 1933–41*. Translated by Martin Chalmers. London: Phoenix, 2003.
———. *I Will Bear Witness: A Diary of the Nazi Years, 1942–1945*. Translated by Martin Chalmers. Modern Library paperback ed. New York: Modern Library, 2001.
———. *The Lesser Evil: The Diaries of Victor Klemperer 1945–1959*. Translated by Martin Chalmers. London: Phoenix, 2004.

Klimt, Gustav. *Portrait of Adele Bloch-Bauer I: The Woman in Gold*. 1907. Oil, silver, and gold on canvas, 54 x 54 in. Neue Gallerie. https://www.neuegalerie.org/content/gustav-klimt-and-adele-bloch-bauer-woman-gold.

Kurosawa, Akira, dir. *Yojimbo*. 1961.

Lacan, Jacques. "Aggressiveness and Psychoanalysis." In *Écrits: The First Complete Edition in English*, translated by Bruce Fink, 82–124. New York: W. W. Norton, 2007.

———. *Anxiety: 1962–1963, Book X*. Translated by Cormac Gallagher. X, 1963.

———. *The Ethics of Psychoanalysis, 1959–1960, Book VII*, vol. 7. Edited by Jacques-Alain Miller. Translated by Dennis Porter. *The Seminar of Jacques Lacan, VII*. New York: W. W. Norton, 1997.

———. *On Feminine Sexuality: The Limits of Love and Knowledge*, vol. 20. Translated by Jacques Alain Miller. *The Seminar of Jacques Lacan, XX*. New York: W. W. Norton, 1999.

———. *The Four Fundamental Concepts of Psychoanalysis*. Translated by Jacques-Alain Miller. *The Seminar of Jacques Lacan, Seminar XI*. New York: WW Norton, 1998.

———. "L'étourdit." *Autres Écrits*, 1973, 449–95.

———. *The Other Side of Psychoanalysis*, vol. 17. Translated by Jacques-Alain Miller. *The Seminar of Jacques Lacan, Seminar XVII*. New York: W. W. Norton, 2007.

———. "Petit Discours Aux Psychiatres." Cercle d'Études, November 10, 1967. http://ali-aix-salon.com/J.Lacan%20Conf.%20sur%20la%20Psychanalyse%20et%20formation%20psychiatre%201967.pdf.

———. *The Psychoanalytic Act: 1967–1968, Book XV*. Translated by Cormac Gallagher. *Seminar XV*, 1968.

———. "On Psychoanalytic Discourse." Translated by Jack Stone. *La Salmandra*, 1978, 32–55.

———. *The Sinthome: The Seminar of Jacques Lacan, Book XXIII*. 1st ed. Malden, MA: Polity, 2016.

———. "The Splendor of Antigone." In *The Ethics of Psychoanalysis: 1959–1960*, 243–56. *The Seminar of Jacques Lacan, VII*. New York: W. W. Norton, 1978.

Lagnado, Lucette, and Sheila Cohn Dekel. *Children of the Flames: Dr. Josef Mengele and the Untold Story of the Twins of Auschwitz*. New York: Penguin Books, 1992.

Lang, Fritz, dir. *The Testament of Dr. Mabuse*, 1933.

Lanzmann, Claude, dir. *Shoah*. 1985.

Lichtblau, Eric. "In Cold War, U.S. Spy Agencies Used 1,000 Nazis." *New York Times*. October 26, 2014.

Lifton, Robert Jay. *The Nazi Doctors: Medical Killing and the Psychology of Genocide*. New York: Basic Books, 2017.

Lipovetsky, Gilles, and Sébastien Charles. *Hypermodern Times*. Cambridge: Polity, 2005.

MacCannell, Juliet Flower. *The Hysteric's Guide to the Future Female Subject*. Minneapolis: University of Minnesota Press, 2000.

Mailer, Norman. "The Mary McCarthy Case." *The New York Review of Books*, October 17, 1963.

Martinson, Jane. "American Girl Is Beating Barbie—and I'm Celebrating." *The Guardian*, July 22, 2013.

Masschelein, Anneleen. *Unconcept: The Freudian Uncanny in Late-Twenieth-Century Theory*. Albany: SUNY, 2012.

McCarthy, Mary. *The Group*. New York: Harcourt, Brace & World, 1991.

McGowan, Todd. *Capitalism and Desire: The Psychic Cost of Free Markets*. New York: Columbia University Press, 2016.

———. *The End of Dissatisfaction? Jacques Lacan and the Emerging Society of Enjoyment*. SUNY Series in Psychoanalysis and Culture. Albany: State University of New York Press, 2004.

Mikhalkov, Nikita, dir. *12*. 2007.

Miller, Jacques-Alain. "A Reading of the Seminar From an Other to the Other II." Translated by Barbara P. Fulks. *Lacanian Ink* 30 (2007): 8–63.

Minnich, Elizabeth Kamarck. "Hannah Arendt: Thinking as We Are." In *Between Women: Biographers, Novelists, Critics, Teachers, and Artists Write about Their Work on Women*, edited by Carol Ascher, Louise A. DeSalvo, and Sara Ruddick, 171–85. Boston: Beacon Press, 1984.

Monteilhet, Hubert. *Return from the Ashes*. Panther, 1965.

Murray, Hannah, Christopher Merritt, and Nick Grey. "Returning to the Scene of the Trauma in PTSD Treatment? Why, How and When?" *The Cognitive Behaviour Therapist* 8 (2015). https://doi.org/10.1017/S1754470X15000677.

Mutzenbacher, Josefine. *Josefine Mutzenbacher oder Die Geschichte einer Wienerischen Dirne von ihr selbst erzählt*. Erscheinungsort nicht ermittelbar: Verlag nicht ermittelbar, 1906.

Nemes, László, dir. *Son of Saul*. 2015. http://www.imdb.com/title/tt3808342/.

Neue Galerie New York. "Gustav Klimt and Adele Bloch-Bauer: The Woman in Gold. Exhibition April 2–September 7, 2015." Neue Galerie, 2015. http://www.neuegalerie.org/content/gustav-klimt-and-adele-bloch-bauer-woman-gold.

Nietzsche, Friedrich Wilhelm. "On Old and New Tablets." In *Thus Spoke Zarathustra a Book for All and None*, translated by Adrian Del Caro, 156–72. Cambridge: Cambridge University Press, 2012.

O'Connor, Anne Marie. *The Lady in Gold: The Extraordinary Tale of Gustav Klimt's Masterpiece, "Portrait of Adele Bloch-Bauer."* New York: Vintage, 2015.

Osgood, Kelsey. "Before Bambi, There Was Josephine: Felix Salten's Erotic Literature." *The American Reader*. Accessed August 22, 2018. http://theamericanreader.com/before-bambi-there-was-josefine/.

Otto, Rudolf. *The Idea of the Holy*. Translated by John Wilfred Harvey. New York: Penguin Books, 1959.

Perlson, Hili. "Bavaria Kept Nazi-Looted Art in Museums." Artnet News, June 28, 2016. https://news.artnet.com/art-world/germany-returned-nazi-looted-art-nazi-families-530786.

Petzold, Christian, dir. *Phoenix*. 2014. http://www.imdb.com/title/tt2764784/.

Puenzo, Lucía, dir. *The German Doctor*. 2014. http://www.imdb.com/title/tt1847746/.

———. *Wakolda*. Translated by David William Foster. London: Hesperus Press, 2014.

Rayor, Diane J. *The Homeric Hymns*. Berkeley: University of California Press, 2014.

Reed, Christopher. "Hubertus Czernin." *The Guardian*, July 3, 2006.

Ring, Jennifer. *The Political Consequences of Thinking: Gender and Judaism in the Work of Hannah Arendt*. Albany: State University of New York Press, 1998.

Romney, Jonathan. "Christian Petzhold: The Berlin School's Prime Exponent of Spectral Modernity Raises the Dead Once Again with Phoenix." *Film Comment* 51, no. 4 (2015): 28.

Rossellini, Roberto, dir. *Germany Year Zero*. 1948.

Ruti, Mari. *Between Levinas and Lacan: Self, Other, Ethics*. New York: Bloomsbury Academic, 2015.

Salecl, Renata. *On Anxiety*. London: Routledge, 2006.

Salten, Felix, and Marix Verlag. *Bambi: Eine Lebensgeschichte aus dem Walde*. Wiesbaden, Germany: Verlagshaus, 2016.

Santner, Eric L. *The Royal Remains: The People's Two Bodies and the Endgames of Sovereignty*. Chicago: University of Chicago Press, 2011.

Schlöndorff, Volker, and Margarethe von Trotta, dir. *The Lost Honor of Katharina Blum*. 1975.

Schor, Juliet. *The Overworked American: The Unexpected Decline of Leisure*. New York: Basic Books, 2000.

Schor, Juliet B. *The Overspent American: Why We Want What We Don't Need*. New York, NY: HarperPerennial, 2010.

Shakespeare, William. *A Midsummer Night's Dream*, 2006.

Shakespeare, William, and John Roe. *The Poems: Venus and Adonis, the Rape of Lucrece, the Phoenix and the Turtle, the Passionate Pilgrim, A Lover's Complaint : Updated Edition*. Cambridge: Cambridge University Press, 2012.

Shay, Jonathan. *Odysseus in America: Combat Trauma and the Trials of Homecoming*. New York: Scribner, 2002.

Siegel, Don, dir. *The Beguiled*. 1971.

Stein, Gertrude. *Everybody's Autobiography*. Boston: Exact Change, 2014.

Steiner, George, interview by Ronald Sharp. "George Steiner, The Art of Criticism No. 2." *The Paris Review* 137 (1995): 43–102.

———. *Language and Silence: Essays on Language, Literature, and the Inhuman*. New York: Atheneum, 1967.

Thompson, J. Lee, dir. *Return from the Ashes*. 1966.

Toole, John Kennedy. *A Confederacy of Dunces*. New York: Penguin Books, 2016.

Trotta, Margarethe von, dir. *Hannah Arendt*. 2013.

Turner, Terrence, dir. *Adele's Wish*. 2008. http://www.imdb.com/title/tt3706976/.

Vogel, Carol. "Lauder Pays $135 Million, a Record, for a Klimt Portrait." *New York Times*, June 19, 2006.

Wajcman, Gérard. "Desublimation." *Lacanian Ink* 29 (2007): 86–113.

Weigel, Moira. "Heritage Girl Crush: On 'Hannah Arendt,'" July 16, 2013. http://lareviewofbooks.org/essay/heritage-girl-crush-on-hannah-arendt/.

Wieden, Anja. "Writing Resistance: Anonyma's Narration of Rape in *A Woman in Berlin*." *Women in German Yearbook: Feminist Studies in German Literature & Culture* 32 (2016): 25–49.

Wilder, Billy, dir. *A Foreign Affair*. Paramount, 1948.

———, dir. *Double Indemnity*. 1944.

Witt, Michael. *Jean-Luc Godard, Cinema Historian*. Bloomington: Indiana University Press, 2013.

Žižek, Slavoj. "The Dreams of Others." *In These Times*, May 18, 2007. http://inthesetimes.com/article/3183/the_dreams_of_others.

———. *Refugees, Terror and Other Troubles with the Neighbors: Against the Double Blackmail*. Brooklyn, NY: Melville House, 2016.

———. *Welcome to the Desert of the Real! Five Essays on 11 September and Related Dates*. London ; New York: Verso, 2002.

Index

About the Authors

Jessica Datema, PhD, is an associate professor of literature at Bergen Community College with a PhD in Comparative Literature and an MA in Philosophy from Binghamton University (SUNY 2003). Recently, Dr. Datema also received a creative writing certificate for studies accomplished at the University of Cambridge in the UK (2014). Datema has published poetry and written articles on modernism, psychoanalysis, and literary theory. She coedited the book *Wretched Refuge: Immigrants and Itinerants in the Postmodern*. Her current book project is a work of creative nonfiction.

Manya Steinkoler, PhD, is a practicing psychoanalyst in New York and teaches English and Film at Borough of Manhattan Community College. She is the coauthor and editor of *Lacan, Comedy and Psychoanalysis* (Cambridge 2016) and *Lacan on Madness: Madness Yes You Can't*, with Patricia Gherovici. She is on the editorial board of *La Clinique Lacanienne* (Paris) and *Division Review* (New York). She has published articles internationally on psychoanalysis, film, and literary studies.

www.ingramcontent.com/pod-product-compliance
Ingram Content Group UK Ltd.
Pitfield, Milton Keynes, MK11 3LW, UK
UKHW040910190926
475560UK00008B/143

9 781498 592970